Stop Overthinking

How to Start Positive New Habits Based on Action and Eliminate Anxiety and Negative Thinking, Declutter you Mind, Reduce Stress, Gain Better Results in Business and Life

Table of Content

Introduction

Congratulations on downloading ***Stop Overthinking****: Tools to Improve Your Quality of Life* by Ryan Goldman, author of *Emotional Intelligence 2.0* and *Enneagram.* Thank you for doing so.

The following chapters will discuss what is overthinking and how it might be affecting your life. This is an interactive book and, in each chapter, you will be asked to do exercise. The goal is to create an action plan to guide you through changes and help you measure your progress.

You will need a few simple tools to help you with your work. We are going low tech. You need notebook or pad of paper, pen (no erasing, cross through and change), file folder, private place to store materials if you have curious household members, and a tote to carry your notebook with you to work and when running errands.

Chapter 1 introduces the definition of overthinking and the difference between overthinking and an anxiety disorder. Common signs of anxiety caused by overthinking are listed in this chapter along with some examples of the toxic relationships that may form when two over-thinkers collide. Self-help vs. Counseling is also discussed in this first chapter.

Chapter 2 gets us started with a background survey. Take your time working on the exercises in this book. It is important that you be honest with yourself if you wish to improve your overall mental health. Please do every exercise in this book as we will be using them to create your action plan. The next two more exercises teach you how to analyze what type of loop is running through your head and what is at the heart of that concern. Emotional triggers and working with your physician are also topics of discussion.

Chapter 3 explains core values there is an exercise to determine how satisfied you are with your maintenance in these areas. Types of worriers are described in this chapter along with a third type of worry loop.

Chapter 4 introduces problem-solving strategies such as journaling, listing, and recognizing avoidance tactics. Coping mechanisms for lack of sleep, failed friendships, and stressed relationships are discussed in this chapter.

Chapter 5 concentrates on reducing stress in your daily life. This chapter is packed with information and ideas. Issues like dealing with clutter, eating habits, self-medicating, and exercise for starters. Then it moves on to a discussion of depression and the physical effects of overthinking ending in a discussion of fear of failure and self-sabotage.

Chapter 6 pulls all the above exercises, surveys, and journal information together to develop a fix list, calendar, and the final action plan.

Chapter 7 is about maintenance. Adjusting your plan, dealing with triggers on a daily basis, and take your growth to the next level.

Chapter 8 contains all the prompt words, example forms, and survey information.

There are plenty of books on this subject on the market, thanks again for choosing this one! Every effort was made to ensure it is full of as much useful information as possible, please enjoy!

Chapter 1: What is Overthinking?

~ Anxiety is the dizziness of freedom. ~

- Soren Kierkegaard, the Concept of Anxiety: A Simple Psychologically Orienting Deliberation on the Dogmatic Issue of Hereditary Sin

Is overthinking a disorder or an anxiety disorder?

The easy answer is no, overthinking is not a mental disorder. Overthinking is a term that means a person spends too long thinking and worrying about certain issues or situations. He or she gets stuck thinking about a problem or situation instead of putting that time and energy into a resolution or moving on. This can lead to a feeling of anxiety and depression if not addressed.

Overthinking can be a symptom of some anxiety disorders, but it can also be a sign of simply being overwhelmed. Sometimes a nudge or taking an alternate path is needed to get moving again. But it's really difficult to nudge your own self out of a slump or find an alternate path never traveled. That is where this book can help you. We are going to review different exercises and techniques for recognizing and dealing with emotional stress.

Everyone, at different times in their lives, has felt anxious or nervous about facing stressful situations. Taking final exams, speaking in front of a crowd, meeting new people, and dating are examples of a few stress-inducing activities. People can also overthink situations like major purchases (car, home, or boat), changing careers, new relationship, or how children should spend the summer. That does not necessarily lead to chronic overthinking or any anxiety disorder. It's normal to be stressed about some of life's events.

Construction Ahead!

Getting control of overthinking is all about creating safe places for you - both physically and emotionally. Building confidence in your abilities to express emotions, learn to handle differences before they build into confrontational situations, and feel free to set new exciting goals for your life.

This is not going to happen overnight. For one thing, you have to learn why you overthink certain problems and/or situations. Then, you must learn how to break the habits that feed the overthinking. It is said that it takes seventeen days to break a habit. But those of us who have had to quit smoking or drinking, or some other destructive habit know it is something we deal with on a daily bases.

Does that thought of dealing with something on a daily bases upset up? Does it drain your energy or stop you dead in your tracks from trying to change a habit?

Turn those thoughts around. Do it right now. You are going to learn to use each day to improve your coping skills to keep you on track to attain your goals. That is exciting! Each day you have a chance to add on to your life and enhance it in any direction you choose.

This is a process you can share with the entire family after you have mastered the skills. When you are having a conflict with a child, spouse, or other loved one, you will be able to decide just how you want to resolve the situation. Rather than the same old routine of bickering or procrastinating you will be able to take decisive action and for the most part avoid anxiety-producing stress.

Think of this as a user's manual for daily maintenance. Follow the directions, put in the work to complete the exercises, and your life will run smoother. Who doesn't want that? Every day you are constructing a better version of yourself.

Blue Prints for Life

If someone plunked a computer down in front of you and said: "Fix this please, it stopped working." Unless you're a hardware technician you probably wouldn't know where to start without some sort of Care and Maintenance manual. Well, the same goes for overthinking. Most folks think they are being helpful, giving you practical advice when they say something like "just stop thinking about it", or "think about something else, instead" or "just let it go." As if it's that easy. Click, flip the thought switch to off and move on.

Would that it was that simple. Eventually, you do have to "let it go", but first you must learn how to do that with success and confidence. For some, reading this book and doing the exercises will be enough to help break old, harmful habits, and build new, life-enhancing habits.

For others, you may find that these exercises lead you to realize that some professional counseling is a better option. When you discuss the health portion of the action plan with your physician, he might suggest treatment that will help you achieve your goals even faster.

~ Don't worry if people think you're crazy. You are crazy. You have that kind of intoxicating insanity that lets other people dream outside of the lines and become who they're destined to be. ~
- Jennifer Elisabeth, Born Ready: Unleash Your Inner Dream Girl

Before we move on with our explanation of overthinking let's look briefly at anxiety disorders and make a clear distinction between the two.

Some common anxiety disorders include:

- ***Panic disorder***: This may also be referred to as a *panic attack* or an *anxiety attack*. A panic attack can sometimes feel like a heart attack due to similar symptoms. You may feel a rapid or irregular heartbeat, accompanied by sweating and chest pains. If you ever experience this call 911 emergency. You can't really tell the difference between a panic attack and an actual heart attack.

- ***Social anxiety disorder***: Also referred to as a *social phobia*. You may feel worried and self-conscious about daily social situations such as after-work gatherings, club meetings, holiday parties, social gatherings with work colleagues, or friends and family. The feeling that others are judging you or an overwhelming fear of being embarrassed or ridiculed at social gatherings is also a sign of this disorder.

- ***Generalized anxiety disorder***: Excessive tension and worry with little or no reason. A constant feeling of doom when you know that there are no current events that should cause this feeling.

- ***Specific phobias***: Fear of animals, heights, small closed-in places, or certain objects or situations. These fears can become so overwhelming that you start to avoid activities in your life.

If you or someone you love find any of the above disorders affecting your daily life. If the anxiety is preventing you from having close friends, dating, participating in hobbies, isolating you from everyday life events, please seek counseling. Don't let something that is easily corrected steal another day of your life. We will speak more about counseling later in this chapter.

Overthinking & Relationships

There are specific signs that can alert you to the fact that you or someone you love overthink issues and situations. Before we review the list of behavior that can signal to overthink, let's look at an example of other behaviors that can snare an over-thinker.

Think about recent conversations you have had with friends or family. Do you tend to somehow always work the conversation around to the same several topics? Perhaps you discuss them at length but never seem to find a solution? Or, you may find yourself discussing other friend's issues, wondering why he or she put up with a certain situation. You two are great at solving other people's problems, but not your own. This type of revisiting of the same topics can be a sign of two over-thinkers working together. Be on the lookout for the signs of the following types of relationships. The dynamics can add to problems with overthinking.

The Independent Relationship

This type of relationship can be problematic for people who have been single for quite a while and are used to fending for themselves. Women in particular who have battled their way up the corporate ladder or are making a living in what is seen as a male-centric career. This person is used to getting the job done on time and under budget. No waiting for the door to be open, discussing where to go, or what to do. This is a person who is used to being in charge because it is his or her job.

Unfortunately, that's not what you want to call your strongest quality for friendship or a romantic relationship. This person needs to learn the art of compromise, selflessness, and sacrifice. Yes, independence is good. You want your partner to be able to function when you are not around. But total independence is a sign of rough roads ahead.

Co-Dependency

Quite the opposite of the Independent Relationship is the Co-Dependent Relationship. In this dynamic, the two partners cannot seem to function apart. It's not a matter of having two halves of one skill set where one person complements the other (writer/editor). No, it's more a lack of trust from security and self-confidence issues. Both couples may have some growing up to do but can't because they are attached at the hip.

Open Relationships

I think these have been around for thousands of years (see pre-arranged marriages), but everything that is old is new again. Sometime back in the 1970s the term Open Marriage came to mean a marriage between two people where extra-marital affairs were allowed and even encouraged.

There is still a tremendous about of debate surrounding this concept as to the benefits. But, for the most part, if you and your partner are taking part in this type of relationship one or both of you are probably not ready for a serious commitment.

The Long Distance Relationship

These rarely work without a solid timeline as to when the two partners will reunite. For example, one partner is sent by their company to implement a project for a period of nine months. This can work if the company is able to fly one or other half of the family for visits. Even then the relationship can be in for some rough times.

If it's a matter of a new job opportunity and one person moves ahead with the other to follow those relationships don't usually fair as well. Typically, one of the partners meets someone else in his or her everyday routine who eventually replaces the original partner. Absence doesn't necessarily make the heart grow fonder.

The Changing Relationship

This relationship is where friends or partners try to change themselves to fit the other's needs. They are constantly adjusting, hobbies, exercise routines, looks, routines, and interest in order to please the other partner. If you have to change your personality to have someone like you, it's not a real friendship or partnership.

Instead of the adult path of compromise, acceptance, and sacrifice, they would rather keep shifting to please one another. One or both of the participants in this relationship need to look at his or her fear of confrontation in the eye and work through it until they feel comfortable being themselves.

If left to continue on to its inevitable outcome the friend or partner bending themselves out of shape will eventually return to their natural self. When this happens, he or she can snap back so hard that they flatten the other partner emotionally. Many times, the other partner had no idea that this person was altering his or herself to please. The change in attitude comes as a complete surprise and the other partner can be left dumbfounded.

Toxic Relationships

There was a case where two friends did a version of what is described above. They enjoyed each other's company and had hobbies in common. After the getting to know each other period - work, family, marriage, divorce, pets, moves, college, etc., their conversations started coming back around to the fact that they had some past trauma in common and how that trauma had affected their lives.

Sharing traumatic situations can be therapeutic and cathartic if you can share, listen, and move on. Move on being the operative word here. But when two over-thinkers get together a situation can develop where they fuel each other's problems rather than help. That is what happened to the two friends. Eventually, they started getting really irritated with each other's inability to move on. Their friendship became toxic, hurtful words were exchanged, and the friendship ended rather abruptly.

These were not two awful people who set out to hurt one another or anybody else for that matter. They both simply had too many unresolved problems of their own to help one another.

Just Friends for Now ...

This is not such a bad place to be as long as both parties realize that's all the relationship is and nothing more. This type of relationship can bring healing to two people who are recovering from bad relationships and are looking for some fun and understanding.

The Dominant/Submissive Relationship

This is exactly what it sounds like one partner controls the other in all things. Another recipe for disaster when it comes to a serious relationship. This is not to be confused with a game of slap and tickle with bracelets and whips. That is a different subject matter altogether and usually takes place between consenting adults.

In a dominant/submissive relationship, the dominant partner takes away the freedoms of the submissive partner. No choices, no say in household, career, money, or future planning decisions. This can be a soul-crushing situation for the submissive partner and anyone finding themselves in this type of relationship should seek help.

Best Friends Relationship

This is not referring to a platonic relationship which most of us has or had with classmates, co-workers, or relatives. A Best Friends Relationship is a term for an adult couple who are fine talking and connecting emotionally, but there is a serious lack of intimacy. Healthy sex life is an important part of any couple's relationship and without that component is doomed to fail.

The Sexual Relationship

This relationship is the exact opposite of the Best Friends Relationship. This is a relationship where two people are clearly looking for sex and no other connection. Again, this is great if you can handle it. I've found that one partner usually ends up with the short end of the straw wishing for more of a connection.

The Truly Compatible Relationship

This is the relationship most of us aspire to. A healthy relationship based on trust, love, and understanding. And it takes a tremendous amount of work to maintain. Those words used earlier such as selflessness, sacrifice, compassion, and understanding are the bedrock of this relationship.

We aren't going to discuss the different relationship types of in-depth, but the dynamics of a relationship are an important factor for you to consider while researching overthinking.

~ If you want to conquer the anxiety of life, live in the moment, live in the breath. ~
- Amit Ray, Om Chanting and Meditation

Signs of Anxiety from Overthinking

The signs of overthinking and the anxiety created by the process of overthinking are listed below. We will be taking a deeper look at each of these signs as we move through the book.

Warning Flags of Overthinking

Listed below are just some of the common signs you, or someone you know, maybe experiencing as a result of overthinking. We will be examining each of these signs in the coming chapters.

- ***Worry Loop***: A worry loop gets stuck in a person's head when a stressful situation occurs, and the person does not have the coping tools to deal with the problem. So instead of taking some kind of action, the person starts to think about the issue or situation until he or she is completely overwhelmed. All the possibilities and scenarios running through their head, looping through them over and over trying to figure out what will happen. This person wants to know all possible outcomes of a situation before you have to face it.

- ***The Mean-Mouth Loop***: This is the little voice that pops into people's heads reassuring them that they are not, and never will be good enough for that job, relationship, skill, team, or dance, etc. A recording of all the reasons they shouldn't try because they know their efforts will end in failure.

- ***Lack of Sleep***: Insomnia is common amongst people who overthink. They wake up after a couple of hours of sleep and the loops start. Their mind starts racing. *How is that presentation going to go tomorrow? What I'm I* *going to do about earning more income? What if he/she shows up at the event?* And as they start running through the familiar scenarios. Then the Mean-Mouth Loop kicks in to add to their distress.

- ***Analysis Loop:***   People who find themselves remembering certain conversations word for word. They turn that conversation over and over in their head analyzing what was said, what was meant, what was not said, what was said between the lines, what was not meant, what was meant between the lines. Then the Worry Loop kicks in to run scenarios and is soon joined by Mean-Mouth to tie each and every scenario up with a failed resolution.

- ***Nothing in Moderation:*** People who overthink have a tendency to see the world as black and white or issues as right or wrong. They go all in every time and don't vet situations properly. This can lead to misunderstandings, hurt feelings, and anger. Which then leads to feelings of inadequacy and self-doubt that can fuel depression or anxieties?

- ***Stressed Relationships:*** Overthinking can lead to friends and family distancing themselves. The over-thinker wants reassurance that they are smart, attractive, good at their chosen profession, witty, etc. In other words, everything their Mean-Mouth Loop is telling them that they are not. This can be overwhelming for the friend or spouse who doesn't understand what is going on and has no skills or tools to deal with the situation.

- ***Blue or Black Moods***: Overthinking leads to depressed moods if left unchecked. There are built-in recordings ready to kick off at a moment's notice telling a person how stupid and unattractive other people find. That's hard to take day after day.

- ***Reasons and Meaning***: What is the point of all this looping? To find a reason or meaning in everything. A wish to feel part of every event and gathering. The person has isolated his/herself so thoroughly (even though it is not apparent to friends and acquaintances) they crave love, attention, and a connection with the rest of the world.

- ***Self-Medicating:*** All of this stress and anxiety can often lead to substance abuse as a means of numbing the pain and fears.

- ***Fear of Failure***: Failure one way in which people learn. While the first try didn't work, correct observed flaws and try again. But someone who is afraid of being laughed at or looking bad in the eyes of family members can stop taking a risk and trying new ideas. They may stop setting goals and end up paralyzed by fear. They can't make a decision to move on, so they stay put and get stuck.

- ***Physical Effects***: Overthinking can lead to body aches from being physically tense for long periods of time.

Headaches and fatigue can result from lack of sleep and all the effort it takes to worry so much.

Counseling vs. Self-Help

Whether you choose to counsel to work through a problem or self-help tools, both paths can be beneficial. Obviously, the self-help route is less expensive. Usually, it consists of a few books, your time, and maybe an art or yoga class. But don't rule out counseling if you find self-help is not getting to the root of the matter. I can't say this enough, **speak with your physician and let him or her guide you to find the help you need.**

What is counseling like?

Basically, it is the counselor's job to get you talking and then listen very closely to what you say. They can determine quite a lot by the way you phrase things. Then they will ask you questions about your answers. It's kind of like peeling an onion away layer by layer. In the middle is the root of the problem.

There are a variety of specialists in counseling depending on the type of trauma you might be experiencing. This is why it's a good idea to talk to your physician for a referral. General counseling for basic emotional stresses, couples, grief, and childhood traumas are some of the specialty counselors available. Sessions are usually about fifty minutes in length.

It is similar to talking with a close friend, but a counselor will point thinks out, gently, that a friend might not feel comfortable discussing. It can be painfully obvious from what a friend is saying that her husband is having an affair. But it is equally obvious that your friend is in denial about the situation. You could bluntly put two and two together for her, but you will make her feel worse than she already feels. There is also a distinct possibility that the information would end your friendship.

With a counselor the client can say whatever they need to without worrying about losing a friend; shaming their family, or revealing information they were asked to keep confidential. The counselor can point out an issue that might upset the client, but that is the counselor's job and again there is no worry of an ended friendship or feeling of betrayal of trust or other stressors that go along with friends and secrets.

This is not a one size fits all solution. You may not click with your counselor and need to find another. There is no specified time frame for figuring out your problem. What is certain, the more you open up and talk to the counselor, the sooner the problem will be solved. Don't hide issues. You will only hurt yourself and waste your own time and money.

~ Successful people have fear, successful people have doubts, and successful people have worried. They just don't let these feelings stop them. ~

- T. Harv Eker

Building Confidence

No matter which path you choose, the goal of self-help or counseling is to gain the skills you need to navigate life's difficult stress-filled situations. These skills are often termed *Coping Strategies* and will be discussed at greater length in chapter 4. You want to feel that you are capable of handling whatever comes your way. Positive feelings and confidence should grow as a result of your hard work. You should also see a support network start to form around you and realize that you are a part of other's support network.

How do you build confidence?

- ***Completion of Task*** - When you complete a task or achieve a goal, you feel better about yourself. You know you can rely on yourself to get things done in a timely manner. This gets noticed by others and you begin to build a reputation as a reliable person.

- ***Measuring Goals*** - Big or small, it is always a good idea to break goals down into manageable parts. As you complete each step you build confidence knowing that you are on schedule and on your way to completion of the goal. Even if the unexpected happens, you have a plan, so you can adjust your steps and still know you are going to reach your goal.

- ***Do what You Love*** - Make time to take care of yourself. No matter what you love: music, outdoor sports, good food & company to go with it, or walking with your pets. Make time in your schedule to do what you love. After all, that's why you are working so hard.

- ***Have Integrity*** - When you are faced with a tough decision and maybe not in your best interest to follow through with the task you promised to complete. Do the right thing and complete the task. Not only is it character building, but it also defines you as a person of your word, which is priceless. You are someone people can depend upon.

- ***Take Risk*** - Don't bite off more than you can chew but do plan out those wonderful goals and go for it. And when it feels like you have taken on too much and you are overwhelmed by the project, afraid of failure, dig deep and carry on. Shove the fear aside and follow your plan.

- ***Don't Back Down*** - Don't let the naysayer's stop you from getting what you want. When you don't get support from someone you thought would be rooting for you, don't let the doubt seep into your feelings. Keep on your path and you will show them.

Sometimes we deal with a difficult situation by burying it deep down or sweeping it aside as if it were "nothing" or "handled." If you find this is the case as you work the exercises in this book, you might want to add some counseling to your action plan. The incident could have been the death of a family member or friend, some trauma that happened long ago, or the loss of a job. No matter what it was, it still hurts and you might need someone to help you through the grieving process so that you can move on with your life.

Route, self-help or counseling, start with these exercises in this book. By the time you finish, you will have the tools to track your changes and see if you are making progress. This will allow you and your physician to determine you might benefit from some other therapies. Don't withhold information on issues and situations that concern you. Without all the pieces, it takes longer to solve the puzzle. Only you can make your therapy a success through hard work and change.

Chapter 2: Where to Start?

~ If you are pained by external things, it is not they that disturb you, but your own judgment of them. And it is in your power to wipe out that judgment now. ~
- Marcus Aurelius, Meditations

Before we jump right into our first exercise based on learning to recognize the signs of anxiety you may encounter in your everyday routine let's do a short background survey. As we mentioned in the introduction this is an interactive book. Please get a notebook or pad, and a pen and keep handy at all times. Stash it in your briefcase or tote bag. You will be using it for notes and exercises.

Throughout this book completed examples of the exercises will accompany the text to help explain the exercise. We will be referring back to these exercises when building the final action plan. When you finish Exercise 1 from chapter 8, you should have actual answers.   For this exercise, I am providing suggestions only, as prompts.

Please complete this Background Survey on yourself. Answering these questions is a way to ground you. Throughout this book, you will be digging into areas of yourself that you haven't dealt with in a while, if ever. So, with all the changes, questions, and memories, you uncover this survey will help you back to center when you start to build your action plan.

- What do you wish to accomplish during the time you have remaining to consider your life satisfying and well-lived - a life of few or no regrets?
  (Family, career, care for others, wealth, land ownership/stewardship?

- If there were a secret passion in your life, what would it be?
  (Sports, art, oration, politics, drama, writing?)

- How is the most effective way to manage you? Give yourself some tips.
  (Be direct, carrot/stick; give examples, suggestions, etc.)

- What is missing in your life? What would make your life more fulfilling?
  (Relationships (friend/love), education, income, direction, discipline, etc.)

- What qualities are present in people who inspire you?
  (Honesty, financial savvy, business acumen, education, strong wills patience)

- What or who sets you back from achieving your goals? What makes you feel undeserving or not "good" enough? What is your trigger?

  (Athletic prowess, body image, intellect, cleverness, lack of family)

- As your own coach, when you seem to be straying from your goal by procrastinating or self-sabotage, what can you say or does that will help you return to your action plan?

  (Forgive and get back in the saddle, do something entirely different and not on any schedule, go to a movie, run five miles, get on your bike)

- Exercise is going to be part of your action plan. Do you have a regular exercise routine? Please list.

  (Run, walk w/dogs, swim, dance, racketball, tennis, bowling, clogging, etc.)

- Do you have a primary care physician? If not please try to find one, if at all possible.

  (Yes, no, can't afford - need to ask for help)

- Are there any medical issues of which the physician should be aware? Please list.

  (Diabetes, blood pressure, bone spurs, etc.)

Education & Action

For our first exercise, we are going to learn to document our worries, the chatter running around in our head that is the cause of this overthinking. The following example seems like it has nothing to do with overthinking and worrying. Well, it doesn't. It's about how to get to the root of the matter. Breaking down the barriers or clutter that keeps us from seeing the real problem.

There is a sales technique called **overcoming objections** that are taught to anyone needing to close a deal. From computer salesmen to petition gatherers. The idea is to drill down to find the real reason someone doesn't want to buy a system, try some new product, or sign a petition.

Let's say your company uses system ABC for its manufacturing plant. It gets the job done, but there have been changes in production and you have to use some tricky workarounds in certain areas. You hear a presentation for a new system produced by XYZ and are impressed with the new features and the product overall, but you tell the sale person no, you don't want to buy. This is where a good sale person will try to overcome your objections to figure out how he can make the sale. He knows it's a good product and will help you make money, so he goes to work.

He might start with the price, is it too high? No, you already know that the upgrade will pay for itself. Is it your old system, are you locked into a contract? Again, no. Is it the thought of the installation process? And with that question, the salesperson has hit the problem. The last install was a nightmare and your staff had problems learning, and the software had bugs that weren't worked out ... and on and on. Now the salesperson knows how to progress to close this sale.

Let's practice. Get a pad and pen and try one or two of these exercises below. You don't have to do them all at one time. Pick the issues that speak to you and see what happens with the exercise.

The Worry Loop

Overcoming objections is one technique that can be applied to breaking Worry Loops. When you find yourself unable to think about anything but the one problem and how it might or might not play out, pick up your notebook and write. Write down the worry. Next, to that write down why you are worried. That should be followed by what action you can take to alleviate the worry. Then work in your possibilities and scenarios that run through your head and write out possible outcomes.

The Worry	Why	Action	Outcome
Worried about BFF Tina.	She is in another bad relationship.	Talk to her.	She thinks it will all work out.
Still worried about Tina.	This guy monopolizes all of her time.	Offer to pick her up or meet after work.	No, he doesn't want to go out.
Getting frustrated with Tina.	She is not making time for me.	Ask her to lunch, or a girl's night at the movie.	No. Maybe next week.
Getting angry with Tina.	STOP		

Look at your answers to the **Why** question, they aren't really about your BFF in the end, are they? Tina isn't making any time for your friendship which is hurting your feelings and making you angry.

What can you do about that? *Nothing.* You can only control your thoughts and feelings. It is time for you to find something new and interesting to fill the time you spent with Tina. You don't want to cut her off, she'll probably need you when her relationship with Mr. X fails, but let her go, emotionally. Also, break the cycle of dependence on this one friend.

Over Analyzing

Sounds like it goes hand in hand with overthinking, doesn't it? So, let's put a stop to over-analyzing before it starts. Don't try to solve your problem with Tina; you can't, because you don't control Tina. It might be a case of co-dependency and she has switch partners from you to Mr. X. It also might be that Tina enjoys manipulating others and having gotten bored with you, has moved on. Or it could be a number of other things.

Note what was good about that friendship. Know that you will find other friends with those same attributes and talents but without the emotional baggage. Remember that knowing what the problem really is half the battle. We will look at methods to help you move on in future chapters.

The Mean-Mouth Loop

No one in the world is as good at putting you down, taking you out of trying something new or letting you know you are going to fail as you are. Why is that negative voice running and how do you stop it? Better still, how do you turn it into something positive?

Let's see if we can figure out where this negative talk springs. We will start by taking a look at the past. Usually, there is someone in the past that took a swing at your self-esteem and made a direct hit. This is sometimes referred to as a *self-esteem monster*.

When a friend of mine first did a similar exercise she discovered a long, lost memory in which her first-grade homeroom teacher was one of her *self-esteem monsters*. She loved art class and the art teacher always had the students sign their work. In this instance, she signed her name in cursive, something they were not scheduled to learn until second or third grade.

Turns out her older brother was learning how to write in cursive and gave her a lesson, using her name. It was a boost to her self-esteem to learn something her peers had not yet learned.

When handing out the artwork at the end of the week, the homeroom teacher would hold up each piece for the class to admire before handing it back. This week, she called my friend up to the head of the class, holding the artwork. My friend was so excited that she was getting special recognition. The teacher asked the other students to note that this student had signed her name in cursive, a subject not yet covered. Then the teacher tore the picture in two and handed the pieces to my friend. She was devastated. Her precious work of art was ruined by a teacher! She was deliberately humiliated in front of all her friends.

In time she forgot the event. But over the years she couldn't understand why she dreaded being called upon in class (all the way through college and beyond) to answer questions. It all came flooding back when she did an exercise similar to the one below. She was terrified of being set up and cut down in front of everyone. Shame is a powerful emotion and can warp lives if left alone to spread doubt and fear throughout all of our thoughts.

Take your time with this exercise. You may not want to do it until tomorrow or next week. Catch your Mean-Mouth Loop running and listen carefully.

When you are ready, with your pad and pen draw the following grid and fill in the negative talk that always seems to derail your thought process.

The Mean Talk	Who was this?	Action	Outcome
You know you'll never finish that project? (Let's say you are thinking about doing your own tune-up on your car)	What project didn't get finished? Who nagged or teased you about it?	Pretend you are writing a letter to this person. Tell this person how you are going to go about finishing this project. Layout your plan.	Did you start the project or go to the mechanic? It's okay if you chose the mechanic; it takes time to erase the negative talk.
Are you going to feel comfortable in that outfit? (you are trying a different look)	Who was your negative fashion police?	Again, write a note to this person telling him/her why you love the outfit and how it looks on you.	Did you buy the garment and wear it to work, meeting or social get-together?

Did you find any self-esteem monsters from the past? Keep these notes as we will refer to them in future chapters.

~ All men are frightened. The more intelligent they are, the more they are frightened ~

- George S. Patton

Eviction Notice!

Do you find yourself second or triple guessing yourself? Rechecking your math or reasoning to a solution? Compulsively checking again and again? Or perhaps dissecting and exploring a conversation or incident over and over? You can't distract yourself so spend twenty minutes or so figuring out what's going on.

Let's take a moment to look at mean-mouth loop what we referred to up above as the *self-esteem monster*. These are negative voices from your past that have found a home in your head. Guess what? It's time to evict these monsters. For the most part, you are going to find that what you thought was a bone-crushing T-Rex is really a little chameleon.

Don't just push the mute button on these critical voices. Silence them forever! We will build on the exercise above and learn how to stop these voices later in the book. For now, keep noting these critical voices in your notes. Whenever an "I can't" pops into your thoughts, if it is critical of your abilities, write it down and know that you will deal with it later.

Talk to Your Physician

It is important to keep your physician up-to-date on any changes you are making with diet and exercise. It's also a good idea to keep them in the loop if you are having any symptoms of anxiety.

Your physician might be able to suggest some medication that will help quiet your mind and enhance the self-help exercises you are doing in these chapters. They are also the main reference source for finding a counselor if you need a recommendation. Let them know about any mood swings you might have. Doesn't matter if they are black moods that last for weeks or the occasional blues, tell your physician about them and together you can figure out what is going on to cause these mood swings.

Do Not Suffer in Silence

One of the biggest fallacies surrounding any type of emotional issue is the feeling that you alone are suffering these feelings. *You most certainly are not alone!* When a friend opened up about some childhood abuse, she had suffered, she was astounded to find that about one in every three women she shared with had a similar experience.

If you feel there is no possible way your dark thoughts and feeling can ever disappear, know that they can. These feelings are shared by many and can come about for a variety of reasons

- environmental, biological, genetic, and more. Don't feel that because you can't solve the puzzle of why you have all this static in your brain that you are a failure or weak. You are strong and with the right education and help you can learn how to take control of your thoughts and emotions.

It is very tempting to ignore what you are feeling and carry on as if nothing is wrong like we do with a cold. It comes, you feel bad, it goes only in this case we are talking about your mind you might just be afraid you'll lose it! That is a natural reaction to wanting to stay in control. Interestingly, when you start to let go and let someone help you is the point when you start to gain control.

When you become more accepting of your situation and feel comfortable sharing with others, I hope you will. Being an advocate and spreading awareness of anxiety and depression will help others out of the box in which you were once trapped.

Find your voice. Dealing with your overthinking and stress will help you find your voice. Below are a few signs that you may not be using your voice.

- Dissatisfaction with your life. You don't feel like you are living it on your terms.
- Others take credit for your work or ideas.
- Often you get stuck with the work others don't want

- You find yourself doing what others in the group want and not what you had planned.

The background survey you completed and the core values exercise in chapter 3 are will be valuable information for finding your voice.

Practice being assertive. Not aggressive, but assertive. Start small with text to friends to meet for lunch or a coffee. Or reach out to a trusted friend when you are feeling blue and tell them you need some company. A text such as: "I've been in a blue place today and need to break out of it. You have time for dinner and a walk?" Speak to others directly. Look them in the eye, show emotion on your face. Speak calmly but clear, not loud or whiney. Stand up for your needs. If you are interrupted and shut out of a conversation try saying "I would appreciate it if you would let me finish what I was saying before telling us your story."

If you are finding yourself in the dumps regularly, make an appointment to see your physician. Be honest with your physician, he can't help if he doesn't know what's really happening. If you think you are having issues with self-medicating and need help with smoking, drinking, or medication cessation let your physician know. If you are too embarrassed to tell your family physician, find an organization such as Alcoholics Anonymous and get started kicking the habit.

~ Since our society equates happiness with youth, we often assume that sorrow, quiet desperation, and hopelessness go hand in hand with getting older. They don't. Emotional pain or numbness is symptoms of living the wrong life, not a long life. ~

- Martha Beck ~

What Triggers Your Overthinking

Most of us are familiar with memory triggers that use our five senses to help us recall memories. The sight of a red radio flyer wagon; the smell of freshly baked bread, new-mown grass; hearing a certain piece of music, or the touch of a Chenille bedspread might be triggers for many people.

Typically, that is not the kind of trigger that is going to cause overthinking or anxiety. We might see a funeral procession and miss our own loved one for a minute, but that view of a hearse alone is not usually enough to cause an emotional trigger.

Hidden Memories

An emotional trigger is an event that causes a person to remember something traumatic that happened to that person in the past. You might be cruising through your day getting concentrating on the tasks at hand and you overhear a co-worker criticizing another co-worker. Now, your co-workers are not gossiping about you, but it triggers negative emotions and throws you off your game for the rest of the day.

Emotional triggers can be as individual as fingerprints, or they can be shared because of a traumatic event experienced by many. Some typical triggers are public speaking or performing. Receiving an invitation to a shower, wedding, or family reunion. Maybe the thought of asking for a raise cranks up your Mean-Mouth Loop.

This is a partial list of actions that might act as emotions triggers for you:

- Someone trying to control you
- Rejection
- Being the recipient of blame or shame
- A smothering or needy person
- A friend too busy to make time for you
- Judgmental or critical comments
- An unexpected sexual advance
- Being left (or someone threatening to leave)
- Being discounted or ignored
- Feeling helpless in a painful situation
- Someone appearing unhappy or aloof when you greet them

Do you have recurring dreams about something from your past? Are you uncomfortable in certain rooms? Is there a smell that sets you on edge? These are all examples of emotional triggers.

Do not shy away from these emotional triggers. The sooner you identify and deal with them the sooner you will feel free to move on. It is better to learn to live with the pain of these memories than to bury them deep where they fester.

As you work on your triggers make a note if you find yourself going for any avoidance techniques such as:

- You blame others for your pain
- You fall back on bad habits or addiction - food, smoking, alcohol, drugs, sex, porn, spending money, work, or gambling to name a few.
- You find yourself getting angry or needy
- You shut down and are unable to have fun or be around others
- You ignore the trigger warning and comply - a people pleaser

If at any time during these exercises you suspect some old trauma that may be holding you back from living a full life make an appointment with your physician and talk to him about a referral for counseling. These can be very difficult memories to confront on your own.

~ The wounded recognized the wounded. ~
- Nora Roberts, Rising Tides

Sliding Doors

The following is an example of a case involving an old trauma long forgotten resurfaced during a home renovation. The old family homestead needed to be sold and the sister responsible for family matters decided to rehab the house prior to putting it on the market.

During the remodeling, the sister was determined to get rid of this one pocket door in the children's bath. The contractor advised against trying a different type of door due to the configuration of the hallway and adjoining rooms. The contractor finally won out and the pocket door stayed with an upgraded look.

The stress of clearing out and selling the family house had led the sibling to get some help from a counselor. In one meeting, she happened to mention the door episode to her counselor in passing, she thought. But the counselor picked up that the sliding door was a trigger for a much larger issue. Turns out a family member had tried repeatedly to get into the bathroom when the sister was showering or on the toilet. She would have to push desperately against the door (there was no lock) to keep this person from entering. Sometimes sopping wet, still in the shower, leaning out to keep the door pulled shut. She had buried these attempted assaults for years. All these years she had a dislike of sliding doors of any kind and didn't understand why.

This is why I will keep encouraging you to think about counseling during the exercises. Sometimes we deliberately don't remember trauma so that we can get on with our lives. Oppressing difficult memories is a coping mechanism in its own right. It works very well for a while. Protecting us from memories that might otherwise lead to major depression or suicide. But, at some point, the trauma must be dealt with or we will suffer even more from the stress produced.

Positive and Negative

Below is an example of the Emotional Trigger exercise. The idea is to get a list of items that evoke certain emotions. We will use this list in later exercises.

Emotional Triggers	
Interest	**Joy**
Music, dance	The perfect taste
Learning a new skill	Playing chase
	Jumping in a pile of leaves
Fear	**Sadness**
Blind dates	Wasted time
Barking dogs	A misunderstanding from the past
Bad dreams	
Love	**Comfort**
Old friends	Salt breeze
Stroll through a garden	Scent of gladiolas
Anger	**Guilt**
Laziness	Betraying a trust
Gross negligence	Gossip

On a new page from your notebook copy the above chart. There is also a blank form in Chapter 8 labeled Emotional Triggers. Write down the first word or phrase you think of that brings out each emotion. If you are having a hard time starting, there is a list of possible trigger words in Chapter 8 below the chart.

Chapter 3: Identifying Core Values

What Are Core Values?

Core values are thoughts, routines, rituals, and manners that you were taught to follow. They are ideals and customs observed by family, friends, and leaders taught to you as you grew up. They are beliefs also called personal values that you usually share in common with people in your social circle.

Core values help guide people in how they live their lives, interact with others, and guide our decision making. Core values are not strategies or operating practices. They are not part of competencies or cultural norms. They don't change with the market, administrative, or political changes, and are not used individually.

Core values guide us in personal relationships, teaching others, conducting business, and in decision making. They clarify who we are and for what we stand. They can help explain why we conduct business the way we do and are a platform for our businesses.

These often differ from culture to culture, family to family, and person to person. A guide will be provided for you, but you are encouraged to enhance and change the example to include your core values. There is a list of core value words in chapter 8 that can help you fill out your chart.

Many businesses and government departments craft core value statements and mission statements to guide employees. They are meant to instill a strong sense of purpose and standards for which they strive to achieve.

For example, the U.S. Air Force core values are **integrity first, service before self, and excellence in all we do**. You have a clear idea of what is expected from your work with the U.S. Air Force when you read this. It is a commitment that each Airman makes when he joins the force.

~ Core Values help those who join us to understand right from the outset what's expected of them. Equally important, they provide all of us, from [the rank of] Airman to four-start general, with a touchstone -- a guide in our own conscience -- to remind us of what we expect from ourselves. We have wonderful people in the Air Force. But we aren't perfect. Frequent reflection on the core values helps each of us refocus on the person we want to be and the example we want to set. ~
- General Michael E. Ryan, Chief of Staff, United States Air Force (CSAF), 1997-2001.

To determine where your concerns might lie, let's try another exercise. You want to be in a calm, clear state of mind for this exercise. Phone off, family in bed, dog walked. Take a few deep breaths and clear your mind.

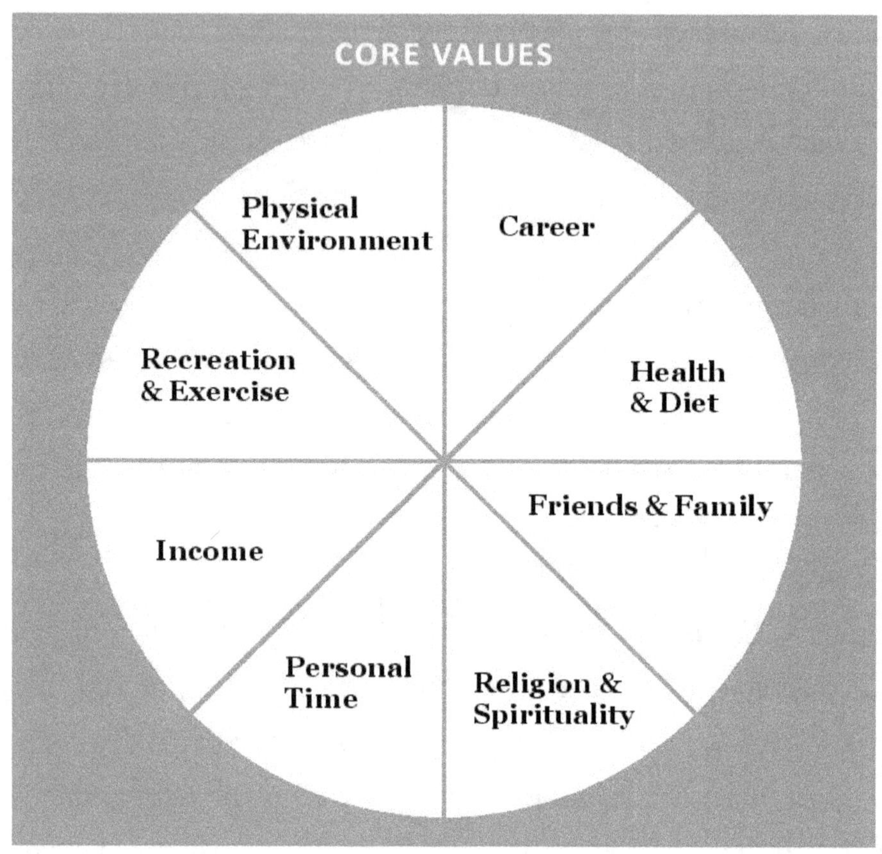

Grab your pad and pen and create a pie chart with as many slices as you need. I have selected eight areas with values familiar to the average American. You may need to add or change some of the headings to fit your life.

You may need to sub-divide some of these slices because I am going to ask you to rate your satisfaction on a scale of 1 to 10

where 1 is totally unsatisfied and 10 is totally satisfied. You might be happy with one aspect of your career but wish to improve upon other areas.

Now let's look at some sub-categories of these slices.

- ***Physical Environment at work.*** Think of the surroundings in which you work, is the atmosphere uplifting? Are your surroundings loud or quiet, chaotic or controlled, bland or bright, energy-draining or uplifting? Do you feel safe or exposed, is there anything living around you (fish tank, plants, terrariums)?

  There may not be too much you can control about work, cubicles and beige paint being what they are. But is your own area clear of clutter and neat with a few items that (if allowed) help create a positive mood to make the most out of your workday?

  Now, I realize if you are a K-3 teacher, there are some chaos, loud noises, and draining energy that comes with the job. However, is it controlled chaos, and happy singing at the top of their lungs?

  How satisfied are you with your work environment on a scale of 1-10?

- ***Physical Environment at home.*** You may be limited to what you can do if you are renting, have roommates, or family who's taste differ from yours. But think about your work and play spaces in the home, inside and out. Do you like them? If not, what would you like to change? Think about your ideal living environment.

  How satisfied are you with your home environment on a scale of 1-10?

- ***Career.*** Is your career moving along at the pace you expected or wanted? Are you happy with your projects, clients, co-workers, and company reputation?

  How satisfied are you with your career on a scale of 1-10?

- ***Health & Diet.*** Are you in good health? Are you carrying extra weight or stress? How are your blood pressure and blood sugar? Do you smoke? Do you drink?

  How satisfied are you with your health & diet on a scale of 1 to 10?

- ***Family & Friends.*** Is there anything you would like to change about your relationship with your family? Too much scheduled a time and not enough quality time? Empty nest syndrome? Stressed about someone else's situation? Lack of input into family get-togethers? Holiday nightmares?

How satisfied are you with your family and friends' relationships on a scale of 1 to 10?

- **Religion & Spirituality.** Are you spending enough time feeding your inner spirit? This could be services, volunteer work, or more time in nature.

How satisfied are you with your religious and spiritual experience on a scale of 1 to 10?

- **Personal Time.** Do you get to take a nap once in a while? Spend time with friends, perhaps without spouse or family? There should be some time during the week that isn't dictated by work or others.

How satisfied are you with your amount of personal time on a scale of 1 to 10?

- **Income.** Are you satisfied with the amount of income you have available? Are you able to save a set percentage of your pay? You may not be where you want to be financially, but are you on track with a plan to accomplish your financial goals?

How satisfied are you with your financial goals and savings on a scale of 1 to 10?

- ***Recreation & Exercise.*** For most people, there is not a significant amount of time available for recreation or exercise, so we skip it. This is not a slice to put on the back burner. The old saying: "The more you do, the more you want to do" is very true.

How satisfied are you with your time for exercise and recreation on a scale of 1 to 10?

Let's see what some answers might look like. For this example, I'm using a 37-year-old mother of two, divorced for eight months. She has a career and shares custody of the children with her ex-husband:

- **Physical Environment - Work (7)** - *not much we can change, but it is a quiet work environment, with working equipment and up-to-date software.*

- **Physical Environment -** *Home (5) - I can't seem to keep up with everything. I'm doing well to get the clothes washed and folded, and dinner cleaned up. The* *main rooms get vacuumed regularly, but the other rooms only once or twice a month. And I never have time for yard work, since the divorce. I can't even think about painting or replacing anything right now while the kids are still in grade school.*

- **Career - (8) -** *I'm lucky to get to work in my field of choice, and it is a good company for working mothers.*

- **Health & Diet - (5) -** *Doc says I'm 40 lbs. overweight. I think I eat well, just too much.*

- **Friends & Family - Friends (8) -** *I have several circles of friends: parents from the children's school/events, some from college, and some from work. Although, again, since the divorce, my time has been limited and I don't see them very often. Maybe it used to be an eight.*

- **Friends & Family - Family (6) -** *Quite a bit of our family is still in this area, and when I first started dating seriously and graduated from college, I had to set some boundaries for my own free time. Maybe that number should be higher; I'm actually seeing more of both sides since the divorce.*

- **Religion & Spirituality - (8) -** for both. *I keep the kids close to nature and their father and his family shares their religion.*

- **Personal Time - (2) -** *The only time I have to myself is getting ready for bed, sleeping and getting up in the morning.*

- **Income - (8) -** *It's tighter now that we have two households, but we are okay.*

- **Recreation & Exercise - (5) -** *Again, time is tight with all of the children's events. I don't have much time for my exercise - those are some of the friends I've been missing. I haven't even thought about vacation, given all the changes.*

As you have time, change the chart to suit your life and think about your answers. Fill out this exercise and set this chart aside in your work folder. We will be using this later when creating your action plan.

How Do You Worry?

~ Worrying is carrying tomorrow's load with today's strength - carrying two days at once. It is moving into tomorrow

ahead of time. Worrying doesn't empty tomorrow of its sorrow, it empties today of its strength. ~
- Corrie Ten Boom

As we have already noted, everybody worries. But you may have noticed that some people handle worries better than others. We've all seen the person who always seems to be concerned about the problems of everyone they meet. Then there are those who seem to never be worried, never show that emotion. There are different types of worrying.

- ***Time-sensitive catastrophic:*** If an event doesn't happen in the time specified, he or she begins to fret. The longer the delay, the more time and energy this person spends worrying. Their worries are overblown and center around the worst-case scenario. For this worrier, life can seem impossible to manage.

  My grandmother was one of these. If your plane was supposed to land at 5:30 and you were expected home by 6:30 - if you were not in the house by 6:31 she started worrying. By 7:00 she wanted us to call the hospital to check for accident victims, it was exhausting for everyone.

- ***Victim:*** Everything is out of this person's control. They have no power and no one understands. They don't trust people, feel taken advantage of and cheated or abused.

- ***Avoidant:*** With low self-esteem, this worrier is a people-pleaser and worries about not being good enough. There are trust issues and this person seeks reassurance from others.

- ***Compulsive:*** This person worries about their work and productivity keeping tight schedules. They are overly devoted to work and set very high standards for themselves and others.

- ***Obsessive:*** This person is triggered by anything that goes wrong or not according to plan, for anyone in their direct vicinity. This type of worrier expends way too much time and energy on things he or she cannot control. It's a full-time occupation for this person. They put every situation under a microscope and repeat all outcomes in their head. You know this person, if something happens on the news, in the office, or even to a celebrity they worry over it all day long. It affects their work, and their co-workers.

- ***Controlled:*** Yes, something bad may have happened but there is nothing they can do about the situation. They carry on with their day even with the worry. Fortunately, we all also know some of these people and should follow their example. They don't let worries consume them to the point they can think of nothing else.

- **Histrionic:** The queen bee, people are attracted to this person's charisma and imagination. Constantly attracting drama to keep people interested in their calling card. They don't want to be out of the spotlight.

- ***Dependent:*** This worrier is worried about abandonment and shows devotion and loyalty to the point of being clingy and needy in relationships. He or she will do anything to keep connected to friend or lover.

- ***Narcissistic:*** This person believes that he or she deserves special attention. They crave admiration and worry about keeping up the appearance of perfection. Status and position are everything and they worry constantly about others finding chinks in their armor.

- ***Social:*** This worrier appears worry-free, but for all their fun and charm, is afraid their risk-taking and excitement will come with a price. He or she is constantly worried about the trouble that might catch up. With rule-breaking and sometimes hurting other people in the process of having a good time, will this time be their last?

- ***Passive-Aggressive:*** This person worries about all the things that could go wrong, or that he or she is not good enough, or fret about how much it's probably going to cost, instead of just getting the job done. Anticipation is usually worse than reality. They can worry about confrontation and speaking their truth to others. They resist their wishes and those of others through procrastination, stubbornness or feigning forgetfulness.

At the top of a new page, make a note as to what type of worrier you might be. Underneath your worry type, list what it is you worry about during your day. Chapter 8 has a list of topics if you need some help getting started.

Type of Worrier: Passive-Aggressive Worrier	Over-thinking Loop	Efficiency Problem	Sharing Opportunity	Possible Solutions
Unexpected bills	x			List - Payment schedule/cr edit card
Renter is not paying		x		Send info to Eviction Lawyer - alert handyman for cleanup - fine property mgmt. group.
Not good enough for a dance performance	x			practice

Lose weight for costumes	x			what are you eating
Practice steps 3 times a day		x		scheduling - can't find notes org
Organize hobby/work/home	x			List and schedule
Dogs need bath			x	teach oldest to bath small dogs
The kitchen sink is always full of dirty dishes			x	end of meal routine - 3 weeks
House needs a thorough cleaning	x			family meeting - ask for help
Kids aren't using hamper for dirty clothes			x	family meeting - other routines
Wet towels in the hamper			x	family meeting - tired of repeating myself
Work out children's savings account with Ex	x			Make an agenda similar to a work meeting - stick to it.
Repairs on kitchen	x			List - order

Control

~ Be not angry that you cannot make others as you wish them to be since you cannot make yourself as you wish to be ~

- Thomas a Kempis, The Imitation of Christ

Analysis Loop

Do you find that you can remember certain conversations word for word? You turn them over and over in your head analyzing what was discussed. Why do you think those particular discussions stuck in your head? Let's see if we can figure out what it was about the topic that upset you so.

On a new page write the title Analysis Loop, make a left-hand column with the following rows: Who, What, Outcome, Feelings, and Desired Outcome. If you don't have conversation churning currently and can't remember a recent conversation, read through this information and come back to the exercise when you need it.

In the example below, the frustrated party is a middle manager with new purchasing software to install across the entire company. Every department for every company will be required to enter supply orders into a central database at Corporate so that the company may leverage purchasing power. Corporate owns 21 companies across the US.

	Analysis Loop - Why are you looping through this particular discussion?
Who:	Executive Committee (all department directors for your company)
What:	The production department has a project it wants to implement prior to your purchasing project. Problem: Corporate has required all companies to be up and running in four months. The production project is going to eat up for two months, leaving you only two months to implement.
Outcome:	Production is granted a go for their project (which requires work from your people to help with software install and some training).
Feelings:	ineffective, unsupported, taken for granted, anger
Desired Outcome:	Greenlight to complete the purchasing project prior to starting productions project.

Imagine how this manager must feel. He went into a meeting with the senior members of the company expecting to get the go over the production project due to the deadline. Instead, the exact opposite happens. Now, some might take that as a vote of confidence in the technology department to get the job done in half the time. But in the particular case, the manager felt he needed the full four-month timeline for the project.

Now he must work through his disappointment and not let it show. Handle the stress of two projects one in half the installation time he'd been given originally. Never mind the daily obstacles that every tech department faces.

Reasons & Meaning

This next example is more of an emotional loop. The sensation of Hear Me Now! You want someone to agree with your vision. Or you want very desperately to have an *adventure* with some friends or a friend, but it is not going to happen. The truth is that you can't force, orchestrate, or recreate good times. You can't make people like you or always sway their opinion.

	Analysis Loop - Why are you looping through this particular discussion?
Who:	Running buddy
What:	10 K fundraiser over in a different county (as opposed to doing the same one you did last year in your county). You've repeatedly let running buddy pick races over some you wanted to do and have been supportive.
Outcome:	Running buddy has no interest, wants to do the same races as last year.
Feelings:	Frustration, anger, hurt, disappointment, disinterest
Desired Outcome:	A resounding 'Yes, let's do something new!'

Get up your brave and sign up for that other race. You might meet new friends. Run into old friends at the race you hadn't thought of asking.

Chapter 4: Problem Solving Strategies

~ The key is not to prioritize what's on your schedule but to schedule your priorities. ~
- Stephen Covey

Set It and Forget It

The advice to 'Set It and Forget It' will come up over and over again in your life. You probably first learned this as a child, watching your parents make not of dental appointments, items needed for a camping trip, and so on. At some point, you started keeping a calendar of sorts. We have all learned if you have an important appointment, deadline, meeting, or haircut you write it down on your calendar and don't worry about it anymore.

The same holds true for these worry loops. When angst over an issue starts to turn over in your head, get that pad and pen and turn to a new page. Write that conversation loop down word for word. Then write down your new arguments, feelings, the way you had wished it had turned out, etc. Keep writing until you have let go of the loop and can move on with the rest of your day.

Always end your writing with a few lines of affirmation such as:

- I can deal with this problem
- I can move on from one-sided relationships that drain me of energy
- I can create my own joy and happiness
- If I don't know the answer, I can find it
- I can ask for help if I need some
- I am making my life less complicated

Lack of Sleep

Insomnia is a problem with people who overthink. You're beaten. All you want to do is fall into a sound sleep. *Boing!* A loop starts. Again, write it down and keep writing until you can't think of another word to say. Tell your mind that this is exactly like the calendar and you won't forget your side of the argument tomorrow when the worry comes back. It's all down on paper and it is safe for your brain to think and dream about other topics.

If the loop clicks back on when you click the light off, start again. Write every word that pops into your head. It might be as odd as, "... I can't believe I can't get to sleep. Why did he say that and what did he mean? Now I wonder if he is trying to tell me someone else would be better to lead that project. I really thought I was doing a great job ..." and so on.

At some point in your midnight ramble, you will hit on what it is that is bothering you and robbing you of your much-needed rest. Then star that line or those lines that seem most likely to be the source of your anxiety and leave them until morning.

~ What you believe you deserve is what you get in life. Change your beliefs and your life transforms. ~
- Jaclyn Nicole Johnston

Listing and Journaling

Many self-help articles and books advise the reader to start journaling. This is great advice, only many readers ignore it because they don't really know what journaling is, or how to start. They are not writers and feel foolish at the thought of emoting on the page.

You don't need to be an award-winning journalist to the journal. As a matter of fact, if you have done any of the exercises above, you have already started journaling. What is meant by journaling in this instance is to write down occurrences of overthinking when they happen. Note details such as the time, place, where you with anyone, or what were you discussing? Did you see someone or something that set off a loop? All of this information will help you figure out what is setting you off and help you shut the loop down.

If you ever took any kind of chemistry or biology lab, you had to keep a notebook, it can be that dry. Date. Location. Time of Day. Record your thoughts, actions, solutions, worry loops, exercises, ideas for changing routines, or a list.

Listing is also helpful. If you don't want to record sentences. List feelings, items you might need to solve a problem, places that calm you, locations you would like to visit, adventures you would like to try. Don't limit yourself, daydream and ride that camel in the desert.

There is a reason your mind is going to this place, churning through the thought or problem. That is what makes journaling or listing so powerful. Give the idea on the page its own time and audience. Come back to these pages in a week or a month and see what they mean to you then.

Much of overcoming negative, worry loops and overthinking is about learning to trust again. To trust your decisions, your ability to cope with problems when they arise. To trust yourself not to barrel down the wrong path with no plan or perpetrations. That is what the exercises and surveys in this book are designed to help. Refusing to work in negative atmospheres or environments. Setting boundaries to negative people at bay. Finding close friends who will not judge you for your shortcomings and will help you with your healing. It doesn't take many.

~ The greatest win is walking away and choosing not to engage in drama and toxic energy at all. ~
- Lalah Delia

Learning to Let Go ~ Deal With the Problem

Learning to let go might be the hardest part of the entire process for some. When a routine has been put in place to deal with a problem, we don't want to change that routine. Change is difficult. Scary. We may have developed some bad habits as part of our routine. Eating, smoking, drinking, etc. All of those are temporary fixes to make us feel a little better about the problem we are avoiding.

There it is, the other shoe dropped. **The overthinking allows us to avoid dealing with uncomfortable situations, people, or facts.**

Let look at some possible answers as to why we are avoiding these situations we find so uncomfortable.

Nothing in Moderation

Think back to our list of signs of anxiety. *'People who overthink have a tendency to see the world as black and white ... go all in every time ... leads to feelings of inadequacy and self-doubt that can fuel depression ...'*

Here is a classic example of avoidance that most readers will recognize.

Let's meet Grace, our thirty-something over-thinker. Grace is smart, has a rising career, is artistic, and is finally taking time to work on her personal life. She is funny, enjoys travel, and is always up for a challenge. Grace puts up a good front, but she is very shy.

Grace started her personal makeover with a change in exercise, which is where she meets Ivy. Ivy is married, has several children, is very fit, and fun. She has fascinating friends, gives great parties, and she makes everyone feel special.

But there was another side to both women that the public doesn't see. Ivy is stuck in a loveless marriage and Grace has been so career-oriented she has no personal life.

It seems like a perfect friendship. Ivy and Grace both like movies, theater, and participate in sporting events. They meet for workouts, have get-togethers with other friends. But in reality, along with the friendship is some **avoidance of problems** by both women.

It turns out that Grace is a great distraction from Ivy's failing marriage and all the fun times with Ivy and her friends make Grace feel like she has a life.

Grace feels like Ivy is pulling away and starts overthinking comments made by Ivy. She starts to feel used like she is a reason for Ivy to get out of the house and away from the family. Meanwhile, Ivy is getting kind of irritated with Grace wanting to be included in everything. Ivy is moving on and getting a divorce, and Grace hasn't started dating anyone.

They are attracted to the same men. Grace gets angry and jealous because Ivy has such ease at making friends. The friendship ends up dissolving and **Grace doesn't understand why it's happened again**. She has been through this friendship fallout before. Sometimes she pulls away, sometimes the other person pulls away. Doesn't happen with every friendship, only when she feels like she's on the verge of being truly happy. Then it gets snatched away.

~ We must have a pie. Stress cannot exist in the presence of a pie. ~
- David Mamet, Boston Marriage

Stressed Relationships

You can see clearly in the case of Grace and Ivy, Grace puts a strain on the friendship by deciding that Ivy would help her develop the social life she had always wanted. Ivy did not ask for or want the job of helping Grace with her anxieties.

Make a list of your close friends and family. If you have that feeling that some have been pulling away, write down when you first noticed the distancing. Note what was going on. Where you at a BBQ, over for a chat, someone's birthday. Friendships take work.

Make sure you are giving as much of your time and effort as you are getting from your friends and family. Give your time, listen to the stories of their ups and downs, and surprise them with little gifts on the odd occasion. Dropping a note in the mail letting someone know you are thinking about them is a wonderful way to strengthen a friendship.

Make up a reminder list of things to think about each week and tape it next to the bathroom mirror or somewhere you will see it daily. Nothing exotic, just something to remind you to remember friends and family in little ways.

- Is there someone's birthday coming up?
- Who has a special event that needs to be honored?
- Extra support for kids this week?
- Planning for a holiday?
- Treats for a gathering?

If you feel like you have a relationship that is strained, and you are caught in worry loops and feel like you are always doing the heavy lifting in trying to keep the friendship up. Stop. Take a step back. Think about trying one of the following instead of sitting and stewing.

Coping Strategies

- ***Plan a Date*** - If you thought you had a good time planned with your friend and it falls through. Don't start second-guessing and wondering what's going on. Either goes on with the plans you had made or deliberately do something else. You will probably see someone you know, or meet someone new. Even if it's not as much fun, you are exercising new social muscles and it gets much easier each time you set your own schedule. And before you know it, you don't need to rely on anyone else because you have a social life.

- ***Take a Walk*** - If you are feeling overwhelmed by a situation. Take a quick walk to clear your head and get your blood pumping. Deliberately find something else to think about during that walk.

- ***Take a Nap*** - Stress can wear you out. If you are so wound up about something and it is eating up your time by preventing you from functioning. Stop. Grab a good book, put on some soothing music, and read yourself to sleep.

- ***Deep Breaths*** - When you realize that you are in the grips of an overthinking moment. Stop. Inhale in for 3 counts and exhale for 6 counts. Do that about five times. You will calm down and lower your blood pressure.

Then choose a method from one of the earlier exercises and try to figure out what is at the heart of that anxiety.

- ***Drift Away*** - At some point, you have to let go completely. You need to acknowledge that you are using an event, friendship, job, to avoid dealing with one or more issues. For example, you may be trying to make more out of your job than is in your job description. So, stop fussing and fretting about your current job and go find that job you really want.

- ***Distract yourself*** - Sometimes we just need to set our brains in neutral and go with the flow. It doesn't have to be a long break, but it needs to engage a different part of the brain so that you are busy enough to break any stress or anxiety and come back to what you were doing with a clear head and fresh eyes. Watch a silly video, take a yoga class, play sports, listen to music, clean something, write a letter, garden, paint your nails, play a card game, read a magazine, good book, or a joke book.

- ***Create*** - Stuck in a rut and your brain is running away with some sad sack situation and you are trapped. Crank up a different part of your brain and stretch your imagination. Write a story, poem, or thank you note, draw cartoons, paint a picture, plan a garden - you don't have to plant it, doodle on paper while humming your favorite song.

- ***Inspire Yourself*** - Make a feel-good moment in the day. It could be as simple as leaving a little note for a loved one or a thank you note for a co-worker. Do something to make yourself feel good. Think of something happy, do something kind, give someone a hug, write a positive note, read inspirational quotes, write down five things you love about yourself.

- ***Play*** - Make time out to play once in a while. You never know what it will lead to, but it will probably be fun. You will also find that you will learn to work playtime into your schedule and that of your friends or family more easily as time goes by. Sometimes people are discouraged from playing when they leave the schoolyard. Nonsense. Living life to the fullest includes playtime. Plan a fun trip, cook or bake, go for a walk and take pictures, skip, jump rope, blow bubbles, play with clay or silly putty.

When Other's Stress Becomes Yours

Another trap to look out for is allowing someone else's stress to become yours. You want to be able to deal with situations compassionately and with understanding. But there is a limit. Don't let yourself get sucked into a bad situation not of your own making when there is nothing more you can do to help.

There are different levels of stress and dysfunction you may experience in your life from friends, family, and co-workers. From passive-aggressive, almost childish avoidance of issues to frightening episodes where someone may be putting their own lives in danger.

Let's say you and your best friend have decided to share a room and board at college. Your friend is smart, charming, and witty. He has a fun circle of friends and keeps everyone in stitches with his antics. What you didn't know about your roommate is that he has a dark side that doesn't come out until you started rooming together. He sinks into dark moods where he won't communicate, is unwilling to clean up after himself, and will not take on the responsibility of cleaning, cooking, etc.

At first, you think it is simply a phase he is going through, and then you start to realize it is a bit more than basic stress of college, exams, and social pressures. You cannot make him do his chores or treat you with respect and kindness. All you can do is remind him of the house rules and boundaries and see how he performs for the rest of the semester. If he doesn't shape up, do not renew the lease with him. Find a new roommate or a new place to stay. That seems harsh but you cannot do the work for him forever. *Suggest that he see a doctor, or that he needs to let his parents know he is having difficulties, but that's about all you can do.* Do not keep trying to solve his problems and wait for him to change. Why should he when you are doing all the work?

Learn when to take a step back and let go. There was a graduate student who had battled manic-depressive cycles for as long as she at been at the college. She had come from a difficult home with a stepfather and three older stepbrothers. There were definite signs of abuse, but none of her friends recognized the signs of this type of emotional disturbance.

The university system was not very well equipped to deal with emotional trauma at this level. And there wasn't much in the way of emotional help for students suffering from any kind of disorder. Her friends tried to help her through bad moods and angry fits, one which included some broken glass and a visit from campus police, with little success.

The student tried to open up about the abuse without much success - shame is a strong emotion and often keeps people from seeking the help they need. Fortunately, she was able to invite friends to come with her on short trips back home. The student knew she would be okay if she was not alone in the house. Her friends were unaware of the violence she had faced at home but knew their presence was a comfort.

Though extremely bright, and capable when she was not on a down-swing, she slowly spiraled out of control. Friends urged her to see a doctor, with not much success. The situation came to a head when the student tried to commit suicide and was discharged from school. Her friends had watched her go from a successful student to an out-of-control person they hardly recognized. It wasn't until a few months before the attempted suicide that her friends began to understand how serious her problems were and how out of their depth, they were in dealing with the problem.

At the time, there was no 911 and mental health was not a topic of discussion for polite company. Thankfully some things have changed and most people have a basic understanding of the difference between the blues and an actual emotional order that needs attention.

Unfortunately, even if you do recognize the signs of emotional trauma, if your friend doesn't or is in denial there is really nothing you can do. He or she may reject all your help or suggestions. You can urge them to seek help, but if they don't believe they are ill they won't go. All you can do is trying, but at some point, you must let go.

You can ask your friend to go with you to see a counselor. Turn the situation around and let her know that you need humoring. You need the doctor to tell you that your friend is okay and not in any emotional trauma.

If you reach a point where your friend is threatening suicide call 911. It seems extreme, but new eyes will be on the problem and your friend might get the help he or she needs.

Chapter 5: Learning to Reduce Stress and Focus on Core Values

~ People think because they employed you, they're allowed to treat you like a dictator, or whatever the worse word for a dictator is. And that's always been a problem for me. Opening the door for someone behind you is as important as designing a building. ~

- Bill Murray

Evaluate Your Working and Living Environment

Whether at work or at home, your environment affects the way you feel and function. You need to do everything you can to make it a space in which you feel comfortable.

Now let's put our overcoming objections exercise to work.

Office 101: Is your workspace clear? Is it clean? Do you have a place for everything and is everything in that place? If you cannot answer yes to those three, then you have your place to start.

Stressed You: I have to work at work. I don't have time to be a maid or my own assistant. I work from the time I get there until I leave, **I don't waste time fooling around.**

Happy You: I think I see the problem. You seem to think that straightening up your workspace is a frivolous waste of time. But what about all that time you spend trying to find the scissors, staple remover, meeting agenda, or your buried glasses?

Solution: *Happy You* got it in one. Bite the bullet and try it for three weeks. Take the time after each project, task, or whatever you are working on and put everything back where it belongs. If it doesn't have a place, find one for it. Clear your desk; straighten your selves and draws.

Office 201: You don't have a problem with clutter or organization, but the atmosphere is drab and depressing. You really only have three choices.

- Approach the powers that be about renovating or at least refreshing.
- See what you can do to create a space in which you are comfortable. Plants, family pics, and mementos can help.
- Look for a new job.

On the Home Front

If you don't get stuck at home and have a reasonably clean and organized house, then there is no need to ramp it up to the next level and go all Martha Stewart in every room. If you have clear, comfortable spaces for working, resting, and entertaining. No need to spend time in this area.

Singles with a Clutter Issue

If you have clutter issues or a stacking situation, then I'm guessing that you have been trying to get your house or apartment clean and clear for a while. *Think back, was there some incident that happened before items began accumulating?* If so, you might want some counseling help to resolve that particular issue. If you've always had a problem where you get shut down before you really get going with the clear out, what happens? Does a loop start in your head? Try the exercises from Chapter 2.

The one thing you never want to do is say: "*I'm not working on another project until this house is clean.*" Because you never will work on another project. Start making new daily habits.

You need to work cleaning and clearing into your schedule. Get four empty boxes and set them out in front of you and grab your pad and pen. The box to your left is "keep and store" and you will need to write down where exactly you are going to put that item. The box directly in front of you is "Give Away" and the boxes to your right are "throwaway" and "recycle".

Pull one of your boxes or stacks and start. If you are keeping an item that you pull from your stack, write down an item description and exactly where you are going to put this item. You can do this while watching TV or listening to some of your favorite music.

When you have finished that first stack takes the "throwaway" and "recycle" box out and fill the bins. *That should feel amazing.* You just made room in your house to breathe and fill with love and positive energy. Now take the "Give Away" box and put that in your car to drop off at a suitable charity such as Goodwill or Salvation Army *tomorrow*. For the last box, the "keep and store" box, take the items and put them where they belong - *right now!*

~ If you missed your chance to read a particular book, even if it was recommended to you or is one you have been intending to read for ages, this is your chance to let it go. You may have wanted to read it when you bought it, but if you haven't read it by now, the book's purpose was to teach you that you didn't need it. There is no need to finish reading books that you only got halfway through. Their purpose was to be read halfway. So, get rid of all those unread books. It will be far better for

you to read the book that really grabs you right now than one that you left to gather dust for years. ~

- Marie Kondo, The Life-Changing Magic of Tidying Up: The Japanese Art of Decluttering and Organizing

Families with a Clutter Issue

If you have family members call a meeting every two to three weeks and work, one new habit into each person's schedule.

Keeping Your Space Clean		
Name	**Date**	**New Habit**
Mom	2-May	Swiffer hard floors downstairs between vacuums
Dad	2-May	Leave work/yard boots on porch stand - use house shoes
Child 1	2-May	Wash sink each night
Child 2	2-May	Put clothes in hamper before bed
Mom	23-May	Don't let mail stack up - dispatch once a week
Dad	23-May	Help fold and distribute laundry
Child 1	23-May	Put away sports gear
Both kids	23-May	Bring used towels and bedsheets to laundry on Saturdays
Child 2	23-May	Put away your games, toys, and books after use.
		add as needed

What is Your Fuel?

~ It is easier to change a man's religion than to change his diet. ~

- Margaret Mead

You can't solve anything if you aren't taking care of yourself. If you have a diet, and by diet, I mean eating regimen, that keeps you fit and trim, wonderful. You may not need this segment, but I bet you know someone who might benefit from a new look at calorie consumption.

I'm going to talk about *macros* for a moment; they aren't just for bodybuilders anymore. Most of the diets you read about these days such as Paleo, Atkins, Keto, and others are formulated around increasing or decreasing the intake of carbohydrates, proteins, and fats.

Looking at food in terms of macros breaks down what is contained in the product so you can tell where your calories are coming from in the dish. Sounds complicated, but it really isn't. The percentages are conveniently contained on the product's nutrition label. For whole foods such as apple or cheddar cheese, there are online nutrient calculators that you can use to figure the percentage spread.

Below is what a typical day might look for a woman who would like to lose weight at a moderate rate.

		Portion	gCarbs	gProt	gFat	cCarbs	cProt	cFat	Calories
Br	Basted Egg with Smoked Salmon on Toast	1	28	13	19	112	52	171	335
Sn	Protein Drink	1	4	20	2	16	80	18	114
Ln	Shrimp Salad	1	16	30	15	64	120	135	319
Sn	Protein granola bar	1 Bar	12	2	4	48	8	36	92
Dn	Spicy Pan-Seared Salmon	6 oz.	0	33	17	0	132	153	285
	Steamed Asparagus	8 stalks	3	2	1	12	8	9	29
	Side Salad	small	3	1	0.5	12	4	4.5	20.5
Sn	1/4 almonds, 1 oz. cheese		6	12	21	24	48	189	261
	Totals		72	113	80	288	452	716	1455.5

Carbohydrates, proteins, and **fats** are the three major nutrients contained in the food we eat. *They are called Macronutrients* or Macros for short.

A Quick Refresher Course

A reminder of what simple and complex **carbohydrates** are.

Simple carbs break down fast and are absorbed quickly into the bloodstream. Some foods considered simple carbs are: *refined sugar, fruit juice, candy, honey, white potatoes, white rice, refined white flour, alcohol, syrups, and sodas.*
Complex carbs, on the other hand, are released slowly in the bloodstream over a period of time to help sustain your body's energy. Some foods considered complex carbs are: quinoa, brown rice, beans, lentils, oatmeal, and peas.

Protein is not stored in the body but is found in almost every part of the body, nails, hair, skin, bone, muscle and tissue.

Fat is a bit more complicated. There is saturated fat such as lard or tallow (pork and beef fat), dairy fats, and some tropical oils (palm, palm kernel, and coconut). You want to keep your intake of these fats as low as possible

Trans fats are basically man-made fats created by hydrogenating oils (Crisco, commercial peanut butter). Check the label for trans-fat content or partially hydrogenated oil (code for trans-fat), and steer clear of these products.

Then there are the unsaturated fats:

Monounsaturated fats - olives, nuts, avocado, and seeds. Oils such as peanut, canola and olive oils.

Polyunsaturated fats: Omega-3 fatty acids can be found in walnuts, ground flaxseed, tofu and soybeans, canola, soybean and walnut oils. Many of the oily fish such as bluefish, herring, lake trout, mackerel, salmon, sardines, and tuna contain omega-3 fatty acids.

Omega-6 fatty acids sunflower seeds, Brazil nuts, pecans, and pine nuts. Cooking oils include corn, sunflower, safflower and sesame oils.

What is the difference between counting calories and counting macros?

When we count calories, we are counting the number of calories (energy) we consume from the food regardless of the nutrient source. When counting macros, we count the calories consumed from each of the nutrients.

This is the calculation you need to remember in order to find out where your calories come:

- One gram of carbs = 4 calories
- One gram of protein = 4 calories
- One gram of fat = 9 calories

The basic ratio your body needs per day is 30% carbs, 40% protein, and 30% fat. Now, this can change depending on your personal health goals that you have set up with your physician.

Sex: M
Age: 35
Weight: 185
Height: 5' 11"
Exercise: 3 times a week, 30 minutes
Job: Sedentary

Maintain: 2472 calories
Moderate Fat Loss: 1978 calories
Extreme Fat Loss: 1483 calories

Sex: F
Age: 35
Weight: 170
Height: 5' 4"
Exercise: 3 times a week, 30 minutes

Job: Sedentary

Maintain: 2091 calories

Moderate Fat Loss: 1683 calories

Extreme Fat Loss: 1480 calories

There are many excellent sources of information for macro meal planning on the web. Team up this method of tracking calories with the Mediterranean diet and it's fairly painless to stick with the regimen. Your physician can get you started in the right direction.

A couple of tips for making a change in eating habits easier:

- Keep a protein drink ready in the refrigerator so you can have a quick 20-gram protein pick up at a moment's notice instead of an entire meal.

- Keep boiled eggs available, they are good on side salads and for a stand-alone snack.

- Fish such as salmon, grouper, and snapper are an excellent source of low-fat protein.

- Quinoa is a versatile source of complex carbohydrate that is good anything from breakfast dishes to chocolate bar snacks. It's not just good for a savory side.

Self-Medicating

Are you using drugs or alcohol to smooth out the rough edges? Does it make going to social outings easier? Or maybe it makes you feel better when certain memories pop up out of nowhere.

To figure out what your triggers are for self-medicating, flip back to the page that has your emotional triggers listed from chapter 2. Whatever form your self-medication takes, think about what set you off. Were you criticized or did you feel verbally attacked? Was it stress over money or a job? Lack of love or stuck in a bad relationship? What were you feeling? Angry, sad, out of control (fear), or guilt?

Make a note under the feeling or feelings that trigger the self-medicating. Put it right there in ink so that you can begin to heal and feel better.

~ A bear, however hard he tries, grows tubby without exercise.
~

- A.A. Milne, Winnie-the-Pooh

Get Moving

If you only choose one thing to implement per week, start with walking. You can do yourself a great benefit in both body and mind with a quick, brisk walk around the block. If you have not been exercising at all and are seriously out of shape, please check with your physician. If you do not have access to health care, start slow. A five to ten-minute walks to start, and then add a few minutes each week. In no time, you will be up to 30 minutes a day.

Not into Gyms

You don't have to join a gym and go all boot camp (there's that all or nothing mentality kicking in). Work more footsteps into your day. Park further away from the store or office. Ride a bike or take a bus to work. Take the stairs instead of using the elevator or escalator.

Many local parks now have Parcours courses. This is usually a jogging trail with a series of workout stations equipped with instructions on how to do the exercise. Go at your own pace and follow the trail around from station to station. Skip the ones that feel uncomfortable or cannot be accomplished at this time.

Wear a pedometer and make it a game to see if you can get to 10,000 steps each day. You would be surprised at some of the activities that really add up the steps. House cleaning and yard work are great ways to get the number of steps up.

Social Butterflies

If you want some company, check out your city's recreation department. They sometimes have some wonderful exercise classes at very reasonable rates. Dancing is a great way to lose weight while having fun. Zumba, Jazzercise, Belly Dancing, Ballroom Dancing, Country, Swing, Pole, Salsa, Hip-hop, and Clogging to name a few. Some require partners, some don't. Most have beginner introductory lessons that are meant to give you an idea of what you'll be doing in the class. Some are more strenuous than others, so you have a variety of fitness levels.

If you are fortunate enough to live near a university, college, or two-year college call them and see if they have any health science classes running for adults. These can be a great way to get back in shape with safe, experienced supervision. The trainers are often the staff and students who are highly trained professionals (or training to become professional in sports science). They can help tailor a workout that fits your time and skill level. You will also learn more about how your body works and what it needs to live long and prosper.

No Thinking & No Kidding

Boot camps or intense workout like HIIT classes (high-intensity interval training) might be a better fit. If you like being yelled at and spurred on to squeeze out every bead of sweat and burn those extra calories, this is for you. You don't have to think because there will be a coach there to do it for you. All you have to do is work it out. These are also usually done in a group setting with a coach leading the charge.

No Time!

There are certain moves you can do at your desk. Instead of a coffee break or a snack, do some push-ups off the side of your desk, or dips in your chair to work out biceps and triceps. A quick walk up and down the stairs for five minutes. Take a long way around to a college's desk.   Make sure you are getting up every hour and doing something.   It is not good for your circulation to sit hour after hour.

Yo No Tener Dinero!

No money, no problem. You can always do squats and lunges across the yard. Get some free weights and work on your arms. Walk or jog in your neighborhood. Start a walking group after work with friends and co-workers. There are many options. You can also sign-up for a local run and use that as a goal for training.

There are so many options to choose from: dog walking, playing with your kids, city classes, gyms, jazzercise, yoga, swimming, water aerobics, belly dancing, off the couch Wii Fit games, ballroom dancing, the list goes on.

So get out there and get moving. You can do this.

Mood Booster!

Depression can be marked by a range of feelings from loneliness to absolute despair.   You may find yourself screaming or crying for no reason. We will look at the connection between stress, anxiety, and the release of hormones and how that affects the body in a minute. But first, let's look at how exercise can actually lift us out of these blue moods and give us another tool to get going when we are stuck.

Endorphins are an example of a positive trigger. Your body releases endorphins and reduces stress hormones such as cortisol when you exercise. Endorphins are built-in "happy pills" people talk about. With exercise, you get a cocktail of high spirits in the form of dopamine, serotonin, and adrenaline. These happiness hormones can pull most of us out of mild depression. If you find yourself sliding sideways into a bad place. Try to stop it in its tracks by taking a quick fifteen-minute power walk.

Pets and Peace

If you don't have a furry friend, you might want to think about adopting a cat or a dog. Studies show that after a stressful task, the lowest stress response tested with the quickest recovery time were those of owners with their pet and only their pet. Even if they had a spouse and the spouse and the pet were both with the test subject, they didn't recover as fast. The one-on-one pet-owner bond was the strongest for stress relief.

Another study reported that spending a short amount of time with a therapy dog helped patients with upcoming operations reduce stress levels by almost 40% more than patience with no interaction. Pets are a powerful source of stress relief. The bond can help reduce blood pressure, lower levels of cortisol and elevate your happiness hormones. And you always have a willing exercise bud with Fido at your side!

Forgive and Support Yourself

Everyone falls off the wagon, it's going to happen. Don't let it spin into a worry loop, forgive yourself and hop back on. Forgiving yourself and moving on isn't as easy as it sounds and requires kindness, compassion, and understanding.

Give voice to the mistake and acknowledge it out loud. Think about what emotions you were feeling when you stumbled. How do you feel now? Like we discussed earlier, a mistake is simply a learning experience. Don't dwell on the fact that you faltered but learn from the episode. Do not allow the mean-mouth to crank up. Being self-deprecating is not going to serve you well. Review all you have done and be proud of what you have accomplished.

Remember the construction scenario. Your past does not define you and each day you have a chance to start new. There was one case where a person with PTSD felt irreparably damaged. This had built up over years and this person had no idea they had a diagnosis of PTSD until a complete breakdown lead them to the right counselor. Learning to be in the present and see themselves as the person they were at the time of the trauma was a huge mountain to climb and get over, but they did.

But it didn't happen overnight. It took time to change the mental image this person had of themselves. The counselor told them to think of themselves as something beautiful that needed protecting, caring, and nurturing. Whenever negative thoughts or images appeared, they were to shield their inner self and not let the negative through.

This person became his own bodyguard and nurtured the small child or flower or whatever he pictured, deep inside. This image helped the adult feel strong an ability to protect himself even though he was left unprotected all those years ago. After some time the image of the beautiful inner self became on with this person's mental image of himself. Very empowering and healing. You can forgive and support yourself.

~ Oh, how I've envied the lives of those who could spend life sitting down. A place to sit, a place to sit! I'd lament, circling my empty chair. ~
- Wolfgang Hilbig, The Tidings of the Trees.

Physical Effects of Overthinking

Let's connect the dots between emotional responses, anxiety, and stress. Anxiety is a natural reaction to stressful situations.

Stress comes about as a natural part of the demands and pressures we feel each day. Traffic delays, interruptions at work, emergencies that wreck our carefully crafted schedules, or chronic aches and pains are examples of situations that can cause stress in our everyday lives.

Stress can be broken down into two parts. The first part is the perception of a challenge which, in turn, triggers the second part known as "fight or flight". These responses are a result of our lineage at a time when our ancestors were on the menu of local predators. Today's challenge comes in the form of an irate driver, crabby co-worker, a child with the flu, or pulled muscles from too much workout and not enough warm-up.

There are a number of physical problems triggered when overthinking reaches the point of constant worry and anxiety. The "fight or flight" response leads to the release of stress hormones such as cortisol. The result can be elevated blood sugar and triglyceride (fat in the blood) levels. Other possible physical reactions are:

- Tremors
- Sweating
- Dry mouth
- Lack of concentration
- Muscle aches and tension
- Fatigue

- Irritability
- Digestive disorders
- The onset of coronary artery disease
- Possible heart attack

As stated earlier, left untreated chronic worrying can lead to depression and even thoughts of suicide. Stress is an example of a physical trigger rather than an emotional trigger. It is important to understand this because a great deal of your success depends on you being about to avoid emotional and physical triggers as you face various challenges throughout the day.

There is a difference between the hard-work ethic most American's were raised with and a constant grind that leaves you drained emotionally and physically. Our relatives worked hard to build America, but they knew how to play hard and relax, as well. Somewhere along the way, we have lost the ability to make play and relaxation a part of our normal day. We work it into our schedule as "vacation time" or downtime is reserved for Father's Day, Mother's Day, or Christmas vacation.

Think about your day and figure out where you can schedule in some relaxation in the form of 15 minutes of deep breathing, listening to calming music, or taking a quick, brisk walk. Do that twice a day and it will make a difference. Perhaps you can introduce a 2:30 p.m. espresso shot club at work. A fifteen-minute break where everyone brings their demitasse cups and socializes while caffeinating to beat the afternoon slump.

Fear of Failure

Shutting off the overthinking, worrying, and anxiety is all about building confidence. We have addressed the meaning of overthinking and anxiety. Completed exercises to help uncover the root cause of the anxiety. Looked at what might trigger worry loops and other stressors. Discussed physical and emotional health and needs. All to build confidence that you can identify coping mechanisms to stop most of these worries before they become chronic anxiety.

Now let's focus on keeping your confidence high when things don't go as planned. Don't let the fear of failure become another situation that shuts you down and prevents you from succeeding with your endeavors.

When you try and fail, you learn something about yourself and what you are trying to achieve. A failed job interview could mean you need more experience or training. It might mean you need to spend more time researching the company or practice interviewing with a friend. It doesn't mean that you are a failure.

Failure can make us feel both fear and shame. What will our friends and family think of us? They're right; I'll never amount to anything - the mean-mouth strikes again. *You don't feel smart enough and can't see yourself in that position so why did you try?*

Take a good look at what you did to prepare for the task at which you failed. Was there some self-sabotage? Did you do all you could to prepare and/or train for the job/task? Touch base with a trusted friend and discuss what you could have done differently. Figure out where the breakdown was in your preparation and fix it. You need to own the fear by turning failure into a positive learning experience. You will do better next time.

Another confidence builder understands what is under your control. Was it a lack of preparation or not having the right connections? You can change the dynamics and control both of those situations. Research, education, and training will help with preparation. Building your contact network by mining your social media network for friends who might be able to help you connect with the right people.

~ Is there a place you can go to break away for a little while? If you haven't yet built your treehouse, it's never too late to start. ~
- Gina Greenlee, Postcards and Pearls: Life Lessons from Solo Moments on the Road

Take a Breather

Please take time out to reflect on what you have accomplished to this point and appreciate the work you have done so far - which is quite a bit.

You have learned exactly what overthinking is and how it differs from other anxiety disorders. You have learned the signs of an over-thinker and how to document the various loops that take up time and real estate in your head. That's a huge step in itself to realize how expensive those worry loops are when you look at what else you could be doing with that time.

You have learned to recognize triggers and found meaning in the connections of the trigger to the worry loops. You have learned coping strategies for getting your good night's sleep back. For shutting off the mean-mouth loop full of negative chatter.

You have learned how to recognize stress-inducing relationships and how to avoid them or set boundaries to keep them at a safe distance. You have learned to cherish and nurture the friends and family who already support you, and not burden them with problems out of their skill sets.

You have learned coping mechanisms for clutter management, keeping your workplace comfortable and welcoming (to you). You are taking better care of your physical health with a better diet, exercise, and a hard look at any self-medicating or self-sabotage.

You acknowledge the physical effects of overthinking and are alert for any signs that may be affecting your health and welfare. You have learned to look at failure as a lesson and speak to your fear so that it does not under-mind you.

So take a little time off to let the information soak in so that new, healthy habits lock in place. Only a day or two. It won't kill the momentum, because you have your daily routines in place for journaling as you become aware of triggers or negative thoughts. After your short break, we will start with chapter six and pull together our action plan.

Chapter 6: Planning & Organizing Your Day to Simplify Your Life

~ Your biggest dreams can become reality, not by brute-forcing the end-goal, but breaking it down into smaller, more manageable parts. If your goal takes years, breaking it down into months and days will let you improve your lot little bits at a time. ~

A.J. Darkholme, Rise of the Morningstar

Now let's take what we have learned so far and put it all together into an action plan. We will have several levels and you will be able to choose what you would like to start on first. You may find you want to handle multiple issues at once or take them one at a time. There is no one way to work the program.

For the purpose of illustration, I am going to use our newly divorced mother of two children and follow her through this exercise of creating an action plan.

Pull together all of your exercises and notes. In your notebook, turn to a new page and set up the following information. What we are going to do is go through each of the exercises and list them with the rank from the Core Values Exercise. We will fill in information from each of the exercises and see what picture begins to form.

List of Problems to be Addressed					
Proble m Areas	**Rank**	**Issue**	**Loop?**	**Emotio n**	**Possible Solutio n**
Home Environ ment	5	Can't keep up with house or yard work.	y	anger	Set up a schedule with kids.

Background survey

The answers you gave here are going to help us prioritize your action plan and may give us some insight into helping to shut down the loops.

- The goal for a life well lived: See her two children through college and on to a career they enjoy.
- Secret Passion: Enjoys painting/drawing. Wanted to be an illustrator. She is a director in the marketing department of a manufacturing company.
- Hint for managing self effectively: Set hard deadlines but keep the mood light.
- Missing from life: Personal time.
- Qualities that inspire: Not losing sight of the bigger picture. Able to stay calm when being directly challenged or criticized.
- Roadblocks to goals: Overcommitting.

- How to get back on track: Forgive and start again as if I did not fall off.
- Regular exercise: Dog walk in the evening.
- Physician: Yes.
- List medical issues: 40 lbs. overweight, not enough exercise.

Core Values Survey

The core values list is also part of the prioritizing process. I want you to use the items that are scored 1 through 6 in your action plan. Anything 7 or higher does not need our attention at the moment.

- **Physical Environment - Work (7)** - *not much we can change, but it is a quiet work environment, with working equipment and up-to-date software.*
- **Physical Environment - *Home (5)*** - *I can't seem to keep up with everything. I'm doing well to get the clothes washed and folded, and dinner cleaned up. The main rooms get vacuumed regularly, but the other rooms only once or twice a month. And I never have time for yard work, since the divorce. I can't even think about painting or replacing anything right now while the kids are still in grade school.*
- **Career - (8)** - *I'm lucky to get to work in my field of choice, and it is a good company for working mothers.*

- **Health & Diet - (5)** - *Doc says I'm 40 lbs. overweight. I think I eat well, just too much.*

- **Friends & Family - Friends (8)** - *I have several circles of friends: parents from the children's school/events, some from college, and some from work. Although, again, since the divorce, my time has been limited and I don't see them very often. Maybe it used to be an eight.*

- **Friends & Family - Family (6)** - *Quite a bit of our family is still in this area, and when I first started dating seriously and graduated from college, I had to set some boundaries for my own free time. Maybe that number should be higher; I'm actually seeing more of both sides since the divorce.*

- **Religion & Spirituality - (8)** - for both. *I keep the kids close to nature and their father and his family shares their religion.*

- **Personal Time - (2)** - *The only time I have to myself is getting ready for bed, sleeping and getting up in the morning.*

- **Income - (8)** - *It's tighter now that we have two households, but we are okay.*

- **Recreation & Exercise - (5)** - *Again, time is tight with all of the children's events. I don't have much time for my exercise - those are some of the friends I've been* *missing. I haven't even thought about vacation, given all the changes.*

Worry Loop

Take a look at your worry loop exercise. In this example, it looks like our over-thinker may be more upset with her parent's than she is with her sister. Either way, what she wants is out of her control.

The Worry	Why	Action	Outcome
Why can't my sister hold a steady job?	She has three kids to take care of and she lives with our parents.	Have set her up with jobs and job interviews.	She always ends up leaving the job after about six- nine months.
How can help her find a job she will keep?	I want her to be happy, but responsible	Talked to her about getting some career counseling	Ended up in a fight, again.
Why won't she act like an adult?	Drives me crazy that our parents let her off the hook.	Talked to my parents, but they make excuses for her	I got mad and stormed out.

The Worry	Why	Action	Outcome
Annual Spring Pool Party	Not sure what to wear this year.	May just let the kids go with my sister or the grandparents and skip it.	None yet
I don't feel good about the way I look	Gained weight with divorce	Tried dieting, without much success	Still fat - duh
Don't want to be seen.	Ran into an ex with a new girlfriend and she looks great.	None stay home.	Stress eating.

Mean-Mouth Loop

Take a look at your Mean-Mouth issues, if you have any. Our mother of two seems to have come up with another family issue from when she was young.

The Mean Talk	Who was this?	Action	Outcome
Are you going to feel comfortable in that outfit	Mom always questioned my outfits - I was a bit overweight as a child. Grew out of it in middle school.	If I wrote her a letter, I would let her know her questioning me ruined my whole day. I spent the entire day worried about how I looked.	My ex started snipping at me when I gained weight before the divorce.
			Now I understand why it bothered me so much. I'm back in grade school.

Emotional Triggers

Again, we are starting to see some overlap of anxieties. Add the issues from fear, anger, sadness, and guilt to the action plan under the Problem Areas.

Emotional Triggers	
Interest	**Joy**
music, dance	jumping in the pool
learning new skills	listening to music
swimming	hiking
reading	Seeing my kids learn - the moment when they "get" something.
cooking	
Fear	**Sadness**
sick or injured children	misunderstandings from the past
getting sick or injured me	loss of a family member, including pets
not being able to care for family	not being able to help someone
not finding a new partner - thought I would be married forever	

Love	Comfort
old friends	kids in bed asleep
laughing kids	the scent of flowers in the yard
stroll through the garden	cat purring
canoeing	finishing a project
Anger *	**Guilt***
Laziness	betrayal of trust
not taking care of family	deceiving family or friends
not being about to discuss something rationally	not being able to save my marriage
free-loading	
*Self-Medicating	

Listing Worries

Type of Worrier: Passive-Aggressive Worrier	Over-thinking Loop	Efficiency Problem	Sharing Opportunity	Possible Solutions
Unexpected bills	x			List - Payment schedule/cr edit card
Repairs on kitchen		x		List - prioritize - schedule
No time for	x		x	Kids are old

yard				enough to help now
Lose weight for summer	x			what are you eating
Organize hobby/work/home	x			List and schedule
Dogs need bath			x	teach oldest to bath small dogs
The kitchen sink is always full of dirty dishes			x	end of meal routine - 3 weeks
House needs a thorough cleaning	x			family meeting - ask for help
Kids aren't using hamper for dirty clothes			x	family meeting - other routines
Wet towels in the hamper			x	family meeting - tired of repeating myself
Work out children's savings account with Ex	x			Make an agenda similar to a work meeting - stick to it.

Analysis Loop

	Analysis Loop - Why are you looping through this particular discussion?
Who:	Ex-Husband
What:	The argument last year when you asked if he was having an affair. You wanted to set up counseling. You had no idea that the marriage was over in his head.
Outcome :	He moved out that same night - to girlfriend's house.
Feelings:	Devastated, anger, hurt, stupid, clueless
Desired Outcome :	You thought it was just a rough patch. How could you get so out of touch with your own husband?

Compiling Your Fix List

Well, here it is. You have assembled your fix list of issues that are making you crazy as they loop through your head undermining your confidence. Now we need to breakdown the Possible Solutions column to see where we need to add help. On our example mom's emotional trigger list, she indicated that anger and guilt could trigger self-medicating, so I'm going to put an asterisk next to those emotions.

Fix List					
Problem Areas	**Rank**	**Issue**	**Loop?**	**Emotion**	**Possible Solution**
Home Environment	5	Can't keep up with house or yard work.	y	anger*	Set up a schedule with kids.
worry list		Unexpected Bills.	y	fear	Put the due dates of all recurring bills in your calendar; try to use a credit card for emergencies only.
worry list		Repairs on the kitchen.			List what needs to be repaired, prioritize, and schedule.
worry list		No time for the yard.	y	anger*	Set up a schedule with kids.
worry list		Organize hobby/workspaces at home.	y	anger*	List what needs organizing and schedule one night a week to work on.
worry list		Dogs need a			Teach

		bath.			kids how to bath dogs.
worry list		The kitchen sink is always full of dirty dishes.			Start-end of meal routine.
worry list		House needs a thorough cleaning.			Start cleaning routine. Put various chores on the schedule.
worry list		Kids aren't using hamper for dirty clothes.			Family meeting - develop new habits together.
worry list		Wet towels being put in the hamper.			Family meeting - develop new habits together.
Health & Diet	5	40 lbs. overweight.	y	fear	Work on a healthy meal plan.
worry loop		Weight gain is causing a worry loop.	y	anger*	Meal plan.
worry loop		Lose weight for summer.	y	shame	Meal plan.

Family	6	Feelings that younger sister is taking advantage of parents is part of worry loop.	y	anger*	Need to let go.
worry loop		Mad at parents for enabling irresponsible behavior, also worry loop.	y	anger*	Need to let go.
		Boundaries have been an issue in the past.			Something to remember.
mean-mouth		Mom made her feel self-conscience about weight and clothes when she was in grade school.	y	anger*/sad	Need to let go.
		Sickness or injury of family members or self.		fear	Write down instructions for emergency or death. That is all you can control.
trigger		Not being able to care for the family.		fear	Learn to avoid trigger

		Never finding a new husband.		fear/ anger*	Increase social functions.
trigger		Laziness, free-loading.	y	anger*	Learn to avoid trigger
trigger		Not being able to discuss something rationally.	y	anger*	Learn to avoid trigger
worry list		Work on children's savings accounts with Ex.			Schedule meeting with ex and have an agenda ready.
analysis loop		You keep playing the conversation the night your husband left you over and over in your head.	y	anger*	Need to let go.
Personal Time	2	Has no personal time.			Getting help from kids will help free up some time.
trigger		A misunderstanding from the past.		sadness	Learn to avoid trigger
trigger		Loss of family		sadness	Learn to

		member.			avoid trigger
trigger		Not being able to help someone.		sadness	Learn to avoid trigger
trigger		Betrayal of trust.		guilt*	Learn to avoid trigger
trigger		deceiving family or friends		guilt*	Learn to avoid trigger
trigger		not being able to save a marriage		guilt*	Learn to avoid trigger
Rec & Exercise	5	Stress eating as a result of divorce has resulted in weight gain and is making you unhappy.	y	anger*	Take some of the time you are freeing up and work in more time for exercise.
		With so many activities schedule with kids, not the time for an exercise routine.			Figure out what kind of exercise you want to do.

Feel Good Emotions

You have put in your emotional triggers for your loops so you can start planning actions to shut them down. Now let's use some of the positive triggers you indicated and set those against the negative triggers. For example:

- When anger is triggered distract yourself with something from the interest column - read a book, listen to music.
- If you are overcome with sadness, look at your joy triggers or comfort triggers and take ten minutes to experience those emotions
- Make sure your work areas at home and at work have reminders of these positive triggers. You have only to glance over at a picture of your kids (two-legged or four-legged) to bring a smile to your face at times of stress.
- Don't forget your positive affirmations. *You are confident that you can succeed and reach your goals!*

Congratulations!

You have assembled a list of issues that have been stopping you from enjoying your life in some fashion. Now let's work on the best way to handle the issues. Using our example list we are going to drill down another level.

- ***Home Environment*** is more a matter of setting up some house rules and reinforcing them until the solutions become a habit for family members.

- *Health & Diet* is going to take some meal planning, will power, and a closer look at current eating habits.

- *Family* is full of emotional issues. Not much here that we can set and forget with our calendar. You can get your affairs in order and write up instructions for a lawyer in case of death or disability. And the meeting with your ex concerning the children's savings can be scheduled. The rest of this is going to need more work.

- *Personal Time* shows the listing of many triggers. This may mean that you are holding all these feelings in and not dealing with them. This is another area for more work before we put it on the action plan.

- *Recreation & Exercise* has emotional aspects tied to the items concerning the divorce. But I think with some work and help from family this can be resolved with scheduling and some discipline when it comes to exercise.

All Aboard!

Knock out what you can right away. Pick a convenient time to have a family meeting and set your agenda.

- Kids will rotate setting and clearing the table each week. Clearing includes rinsing dishes and putting them in the dishwasher.

- Everyone will rinse dishes and put them in the dishwasher after use. No stacking in the sink.

- Wet towels must be dried prior to dropping in hamper.
- As soon as you change, put your dirty clothes in the hamper.
- Volunteer needed to make reminder signs to post over hamper, in rooms, and at the kitchen sink.
- Will meet again in three weeks to see how changes are progressing.

Our example mom realizes while she is waiting to get kids from the practice, she can come twenty minutes early and get some walking in or work on the park equipment. This will give her two 20 minute workout sessions a week in addition to the dog walks. She will also be increasing the length of the dog walks to add more steps to her day.

In the set it and forget it column our mom schedules an appointment with a family lawyer to get a will set up. And she schedules the meeting with her ex to talk about the savings account for the children.

Our mom has also done some reading up on the Mediterranean Diet and has scheduled some time to sit down and figure out meals and when she can cook. Some evenings are too full to make dinner from scratch. She needs to have something ready to go. This will cut down of fast food stops and pizza orders. Her calendar looks something like this. And because she has the kids helping with more chores, she can make better use of some personal time. When the children are with their father every other weekend, she sees she has time to work on other projects or maybe schedule time with a friend to go to a movie.

Already we should have some relaxing of the shoulders and be able to release some of the stress that that was being held in the body due to lack of action.

Sunday	Monday	Tuesday	Wednesday	Thursday	Friday	Saturday
			7:00 Family Meeting	Walk during swim practice 5;00	w/dad *	Meal Planning, Shopping - w/dad*
w/dad		Walk during ball practice 5;00		Walk during swim practice 5;00		Kids Game 10:00 in town
	Meet with family lawyer 3:30	Walk during ball practice 5;00		Walk during swim practice 5;00	w/dad *	Swim meet 6:30 a.m. out of town, w/dad (Get den cleared for craft room org)*

w/dad		Walk during ball practic e 5;00	7:00 Family Meeting	Walk during swim practice 5;00		Meet with Ex 1:30
		Walk during ball practic e 5;00		Walk during swim practice 5;00		

Time to Dig

Now we need to figure out what to do with the issues that you can't put on the calendar. There were quite of few issues in the area of Family and Personal that needs to be addressed. It looks like they may be intertwined, but don't jump to conclusions. There are definite issues with the sister and how it appears the parents are enabling her by letting her and her children live at their house.

She has also mentioned being upset with her mother for making her feel self-conscious about her body image. Who knows, that might also be tied up with the sister in some way.

For your emotional items that cannot be scheduled like the examples above. Start with your journal. Write down what you meant by the statements you see on your Fix List. Drill down a bit further by using the Analysis Loop exercise. Use the letter-writing method to let your side of the story is heard once and for all.

Connect the Dots

Look for connections to triggers. In our example, I see where laziness and free-loading are listed as an anger trigger under family. Again this points strongly to the sister, but do those thoughts pop up when our mom journals about the situation with her sister? They might or it may be that this is a completely different issue perhaps with the husband or something from her past. When you identify triggers in your writing. Use a highlighter and mark those so they stand out. Then think about what you have written. There is probably a hint as to how to avoid that trigger in the writing.

If after several weeks of working with your journal and sifting through your thoughts and memories, you haven't managed to stop certain loops. It might be time to think about scheduling an appointment with a counselor. With all the work you have already completed, you and your counselor should be able to get the situation figured out fairly quickly.

Liquid Courage?

Think about the past several weeks, when have you reached for a drink or other substance to numb the pain? The emotions anger and guilt were the two that our example mom indicated might trigger her to self-medicate. Be honest and keep a log of the days and time of day you are triggered to reach for a drink or pill to help you cope. Put it down on the calendar with the rest of the items and see if there is a pattern that you may have been unaware of or ignoring.

Perhaps our mom finds that she doesn't have alcohol too excess that often, every other week or so. But when she charts it, she realizes that it's the Friday and Saturday night that the children are over at their dad's house. So, some of her built-in personal time is being self-sabotaged by alcohol. That sheds new light on the way she might view some of her issues under personal time.

~ When you do things in the present that you can see, you are shaping the future that you are yet to see. ~
- Idowu Koyenikan, Wealth for All: Living a Life of Success at the Edge of Your Ability

Pulling Everything Together

Set your Fix List and your Calendar side by side. Look at them closely and create your action plan. Your action plan should have enough detail to achieve a very specific goal. You also want to keep in mind a way to measure the achievement of goals and accountability. You might post on Facebook to friends that you are training for a certain walk/run. Let their interest and excitement feed yours and visa-versa.

Write out what you are going to do the next three weeks to put everything you have learned and practiced into work. Be very specific with times and dates and places when you can.

If you need a daily action plan when you first start out, make one. Most people do well with the three-week layout so that they don't feel like they are micromanaging themselves. A quick to-do list makes a good daily action plan.

Example:

Action Plan

- Every third Wednesday, starting this week, we will have a family meeting to go over issues or concerns with the goal of making the house run smoother. In this first meeting, I will set down some ground rules, hand rising, and no interruptions when someone is talking. I will install a whiteboard which will have the main topic of the meeting which in this case is dirty dishes and dirty clothes/towels. I will also ask the kids if they have issues they would like to discuss. Then we'll go from there and see what happens for the next three weeks.

- To increase my exercise I will arrive early to pick up the kids and plan to walk from 5:00 to 5:30 while the kids are at practice. I am also going to invite other parents to join me. I will also increase the dog walks from 10 minutes to 20 minutes.

- I am meeting with the lawyer in two weeks to find out what I need to do to safeguard the children's future.

- I am meeting with my ex-husband in four weeks to resolve how we are going to handle the children's college fund.

- I have an annual check-up scheduled in two months, so I don't feel a need to schedule an appointment any sooner.

- My goal is to have lost 10 pounds by the annual check-up.

- I have set up a time for meal planning this Saturday and plan to do some research on high-protein, low-carb diets.

- I will review my fix list in three weeks prior to our next family meeting to determine what needs to be added or adjusted.

- For the time being, I am journaling my loops and when I feel triggers set off overthinking bouts. It is actually getting easier to control some of them.

- I may need to speak to my physician to find a counselor for this situation with my sister. That worry is in my head quite a bit and I can't seem to let go of it.

- Overall, I am feeling less stress and more hopeful that I can get through this hard time.

Chapter 7: Maintain Focus & Measure Results

~ To be yourself in a world that is constantly trying to make you something else is the greatest accomplishment. ~

- Ralph Waldo Emerson

Adjusting your plan

Now you should be on a role. Handling the unexpected is easier because you've got control of your time. You have learned to write down the loops when they startup. You have the exercises to break the loops down to get to the issue that is really bothering you, which may or may not be obvious.

Whether or not you are a parent, sharing your life and space with someone, or living alone, I strongly suggest keeping the three-week check-up meeting. Even if it's just you and the dogs.

Six Week Review

Look at your fix list and edit to match your current situation.

- Have you noticed new loops?
- If so, are the topics new or along the same line as the old worries?
- How much have you accomplished from the fix list?

- Are you feeling less stress overall?
- If you have family, have you been able to share any of your coping strategies with them?

Twelve Week Review

- Is your fix list clearing?
- Is it time to review your core values?
- Do you see signs that maybe counseling would be a good step for certain issues?
- Have you been able to let go of any toxic relationships?
- Have you noticed any self-sabotage going on?
- Take a look at the background survey you did when you first started working on this book. It may be time to redo your core values to work in some of the projects or ideas on that survey that you weren't ready to handle at the time.

Dealing with triggers

At the end of the last chapter, we talked about looking for triggers in the journaling process and highlighting each trigger that pops up. Review that journal and add them to your trigger list. Are you seeing repeats or new triggers? Are you getting better at spotting triggers in your everyday routine so that you can avoid them before you get set off?

Remember that emotional triggers are a result of past negative experiences. When you come across a similar situation to the experience you had in the past, you can stir up strong emotions without realizing why. The mind has an automatic response to the trigger which could cause an emotional outburst, a feeling of "freezing up," or panic. Get to your journal as soon as possible and note the situation, trigger, and reaction. This will help you be prepared next time you realize you are stepping into what might be a volatile situation for you.

Another good reason for avoiding alcohol or other drugs. When you are under the influence you don't have much control over your actions or emotions. This may lead you to experience the emotional pain of being triggered.

You can control this, leave off the stimulants.

Give yourself a break. When you feel the anxiety, let the person you are with whether it be work, family, or friend that you need some air, or to give you a minute and you'll get back to you on that. Depending on how you handle the response, no one needs to know you are having a panic attack or some other reaction. It's okay to back away so that you don't lose your temper or build the situation into a larger problem.

Take your time learning to deal with the problem. If a barking dog sets you off, ask a friend if you can meet them at the park and just watch them play with their dog. When you get comfortable with watching the next step might be to pet the dog. You may never get up to a game of slobber ball, but you can at least get to a place where you are comfortable when a dog barks.

And don't forget your positive affirmations when you are breaking down anxieties and triggers. You want to reward yourself for being brave and facing the problem. Because as you know, many people are never able to get started. You have taken many strides just by starting this book!

"I can face my fears and get through a tough situation without shutting down!"

When handling unavoidable triggers the best thing to do is face them head-on. You have an unexpected bill (one of our mom's issues). Call the company and let them know you need a payment plan. Planned to cook, but something unexpected happened - it's okay to have a fast-food night once in a while. What emotion are you feeling, fear? Do something very safe. Loneliness? Call a trusted friend or relative and tell them you are feeling a bit down. It's okay to share what you are feeling with others.

Keep items around you that trigger positive feelings. A ticket stub from that fantastic concert. Pictures from your last vacation. An animal to care for and love. Soothing or uplifting music.

There are also ways to work out some of the negative emotions in a positive way. Get out the loppers and prune the trees. Tear up your recycle paper of bills and other mail by hand. Grab a ball and dribble as hard as you can outside on the walk. Take deep breaths in for three counts and exhale for six counts. This will slow your pulse and lower blood pressure.

Have Plan of Distraction ready when unexpected triggers set you off and you can handle almost anything life can throw your way.

Tipping Points

As you being to work changes into your daily routine, you will uncover new strengths and weakness. They may not be obvious at first, so you need to be mindful of your triggers and pay attention.

One example would be a friend who had spent quite a few years caring for an elderly parent with end-stage Alzheimer's. She was exhausted, had neglected friends, exercise, love interest, in short, she had to build her life up again. She was shocked at the state she was in, not having had a regular exercise routine for those years. Unintentionally isolating herself from fun and companionship had taken its toll.

So, she decided to take up a dance class for exercise. It was a struggle at first. She didn't like looking at herself in the mirror. Had troubles accepting out-of-shape body (and ten years older) that she saw in the mirror. But time and determination helped her reach her goals. Within a year she had shaped up, lost weight, and was dancing with a local folk troupe. The costumes were beautiful and made her feel like a princess (something that was kind of frowned on in her family).

She found she enjoyed getting in front of an audience and performing with the other dancers, even venturing so far as to do a solo. But of course, there was a cost. Due to an injury received many years ago she was directionally challenged and had to work extra hard to learn the routines.

The extra concentration and practice it took to learn the dance steps was kind of a double-edged sword. On the one hand, she found it really helped her mental thought process, a great way to rehab her brain injury (which never stops you are always in recovery). On the other hand, it required almost all of her free time to keep up with the changing routines.

This wasn't a problem until she started restructuring a different aspect of her life. For about two years she worked on Health & Diet, Recreation & Exercise, and Personal Time. Having had success in these areas, it was time to move on and work on Physical Environment and Income. She was interested in adding a new source of income to her current job. Really she wanted to change career paths altogether but didn't have the luxury of setting her old job aside and concentrating on a new path. She also had changes she wanted to make to her home, as it was in need of some repairs and updating.

When she started an online course for her new career she found it very difficult to do both the course work and the dance practice. After struggling with it for a month or so she realized she was falling into some old routines that were not constructive. She had to stop and reassess how she was going to spend her time to accomplish her goals. It took a while to realize that the time and effort she put into learning the dance steps was the same time and effort needed for the new course work.

Instead of falling into a spiral of disappointment and losing her grip on every piece of ground she had gained, she took time to prioritize her wants with her needs. She could step back from the performing and still practice and exercise while she was using the extra time and energy to learn the new skills. This way she didn't feel like a slacker and she was able to add a new goal.

This is an example of a positive resolution to the *All-or-Nothing* urge that often hits over-thinkers. Instead of "Well if I can't do all the activities in the dance, I'll just drop it" she opted for a solution that allows her wiggle room.

When you are feeling stressed and disappointed because you can't do everything your heart desires, take a step back and see where you can make compromises with yourself. You will gain much more ground and confidence in your own abilities to cope.

~ The only way that we can live, is if we grow. The only way that we can grow is if we change. The only way that we can change is if we learn. The only way we can learn is if we are exposed. And the only way that we can become exposed is if we throw ourselves out into the open. Do it. Throw yourself. ~
- C. JoyBell C.

Moving to the next level

At six months how much of your fix list is clear and how have your core value numbers changed?

If the answer is nothing because schedules got changed. The new habits with the dishes and laundry didn't stick. It was too hot, too wet to walk or I used the time at work. Then you should seriously think about scheduling some counseling because something is still causing you to avoid dealing with your basic issues. Take all of the work you have done with this book and review the outcomes with your physician and ask him to recommend someone to help you sort out what is holding you back.

Remember, no one can do the work for you. They can only point the way or give you the tools to make things easier.

Emotional scars from trauma can linger long after the traumatic event. Be kind to yourself at this six-month mark. By now you must have some favorite de-stress techniques, such as a bubble bath or time in the garden. Recognize what was preventing you from moving on with your life, such as fear of change or self-doubt, and look at how you have overcome those fears and doubts. Prepare in advance for stressful days such as major holidays with parties, or alone time when you can't be with friends and family.

Do you have more time now to discover your passion, take up a new hobby or sign up for classes? Or is it full of other activities that have popped up because of your hard work? Remember that each day you are working on becoming the best you that you can be.

New Construction Zone!

Building new relationships, either friendships or dating relationships, can be especially tough for trauma survivors. But you have your coping strategies to help you rebuild a sense of trust and allow you to form new attachments, slowly and carefully. You know the signs to look for if a friendship starts to become one-sided or draining. You know how to vet people before investing your time and heart 100%. No more emotional vampires for you. Alternately, you know how to keep from draining the friends and family you already have supporting you.

You have stopped blaming yourself for everything that didn't go exactly as planned. Instead of being stuck in a cycle of worry and mean-mouth loops, you take a step back and reflect on what is at the root of your problem. You know how to smash negative thoughts with solid affirmations. Or take a timeout when someone overwhelms you with their negative energy.

A change such as you have made symbolizes the loss of a relationship namely your old self. It's normal to experience the five stages of grief -- denial, anger, bargaining, depression, and acceptance. And you now know that you should allow yourself to feel your emotions instead of ignoring them. If you find yourself wanting to suppress any of the feelings, lean on your support tools for healthy expressions, such as journaling, writing letters to yourself, crying, and reviewing your old journals so you can see how far you have come. When you feel frustrated or stuck be kind to yourself, these feelings will pass. We all move at our own pass and you will see that sometimes things don't happen as quickly as you might like. Be patiently persistent and you will move along.

~ Sooner or later we all discover that the important moments in life are not the advertised ones, not the birthdays, the graduation, the weddings, not the great goals achieved. The real milestones are less prepossessing. They come to the door of memory unannounced, stray dogs that amble in, sniff around a bit and simply never leave. Our lives are measured by these. ~

- Susan B. Anthony

Celebrating milestones

This is part of taking care of yourself. You need to pat yourself on the back when you make it through a difficult time, or lose ten pounds, or get that den converted into your new art room. Buy yourself something pretty for the room, a sort of house warming gift to your new space. Or take a weekend off and pamper yourself. All of those are positive steps, but let's look at celebrating a larger part of the milestone.

Out with the Old

Think about the discussions that you hear around the New Year. Friends and family talk about diet and exercise changes. Maybe a new job or get that boat they've always wanted. Start the Great American Novel or move to the beach. Somehow the talk usually turns to things they are not happy with (or starts with the - diet and exercise). Why is it we are more likely to focus on the bad things in our lives? Why do we have to work so hard to remember and celebrate all the wonderful things we have accomplished over the year or years?

I don't know if it is buried in what's left of our pre-historic brain that focus' on the trauma and bad news that surrounds our lives. I am certain it was tough being "on the menu" but goodness that was quite a while ago. Or was it? Have we simply change predators from lions, tigers, and bears to deadlines, board meetings, and past due bills? I understand that pain is easier to remember than our feel-good emotions. But for a good reason. Pain prevents us from damaging ourselves past the point of repair. It's a warning to pull the hand back from the flame.

Choose Joy & Love

Don't let the bad feelings have more power than the joy you feel when the soft scent of Confederate Jasmine or Wisteria drifts across your path early in the morning. Chose to use your five senses to overcome the bad feelings. Empower yourself to feel good even when events surrounding you might not be so great.

This book is all about constructing a better life, about how to choose to be happy. Think about what things you currently celebrate in life. Make a list. Maybe it's birthdays, holidays, anniversaries, memorials, and weddings. But what about accomplishments. We seem to stop after high-school and college graduation. Maybe an occasional large contract or corner office celebration.

Make the time to honor all the hard work you have put into the changes that you have made so far. Look at how other cultures celebrate and try something besides the dinner out or the backyard BBQ. Maybe a candle-lighting celebration or a throw and old fashioned tea dance for fun (period dress and all). Do some research into the celebrations of other cultures; invite your friends to join you. Each could take a continent, find a seasonal, ancestral, and life-affirming or earth healing ritual and schedule a party once a quarter.

Love your life, love yourself. Self -love isn't narcissism; it's about caring and respecting yourself because if you don't, no one else will either. Love is the highest form of healing because that is who we are meant to - love beings. You remember when you have been in love. And when we love ourselves, we spread that feeling to those around us. It's addictive, in a positive, healing way.

What about daily celebrations? How about a ritual at the end of the day where you hold hands (or a paw) and state out loud three things you are happy for in your life. Three positive things that happened to help you through your day. Or it could be three things you accomplished or made positive progress toward a goal.

Love Your Life, Love Yourself

If the anniversary of trauma is difficult. Celebrate that day. Turn it around and look at how far you have come in your healing process. You are the hero of your own story. Write a magnificent tale of love and adventure.

~ The best way to not feel hopeless is to get up and do something. Don't wait for good things to happen to you. If you go out and make some good things happen, you will fill the world with hope, you will fill yourself with hope. ~

- Barack Obama

Helping Others

We touched briefly on other people with emotional trauma in chapter 4. But that was in terms of not getting caught up on someone else's trauma and setting yourself back from achieving your goals. Now you have some success under your belt, and you know how wonderful life can be if you do seek help. Let's look at some techniques for approaching a person who may need a helping hand.

As high as one in five Americans could be dealing with mental health issues at any time. The odds of you running into someone you know or work with who are struggling with anxiety are fairly high. But it's a difficult and personal subject of conversation. If you really don't know the person but have to interact with him or her, I would advise talking to your HR department.

If it is somewhere other than work, be polite and listen. If you do broach the subject you might say something like "Yes, I understand how stressful it is to have so much on your plate at one time. Have you thought about talking to someone about it? I've found it most helpful to get someone else's viewpoint when I'm underwater with stress."

If you do know the person and feel comfortable starting the conversation try these tips.

- Find an inviting space that is quiet and comfortable. You want to try to minimize interruptions and distractions. Think about what type of atmosphere your friend likes and try to find a close fit.
- Ease into the topic gradually. This person may or may not be ready to talk and you don't want to make them feel uncomfortable. Kindness and understanding go a long way, and just letting them know that you are there for them is one of the best things you can do.
- Speak in a straightforward manner in a calm and relaxed voice. Stick to one topic at a time.

- Ask them how their day is going, what projects they are working on, or how things are at home. One of these topics may give you an opening to ask about how they are feeling. Be empathetic to their feelings and show that you are listening attentively, such as "I understand some days can be more hectic than others. It sounds to me as though this is one of those bad days for you."

- Try to avoid a direct, lecture tone. You want the conversation to be quiet and personal. Use 'you' statements and 'I' statements instead of a third person example style.

- Listen with intent, making eye contact and let them know you care.

- Avoid prying questions; build on what comes up in the conversation. Or use your own experience with depression or anxiety to keep the conversation two-sided. You don't want your friend feeling as though this is an intervention. You are trying to reduce defensiveness by looking for common ground.

- Give them time to open up and talk, but only if they want to. Don't press for information or conversation.

- Be prepared to keep the conversation going, but light. You may need to talk about events coming up in the community or something you heard on the radio. It may have nothing to do with their situation. Be there and listen. You are trying to build a rapport and build trust.

- Remember that mental illness has nothing to do with a person's intellect. Keep the conversation at a level with their age and development level, never talk down.

- Be aware of signs that your friend is being upset by the conversation and steer to a neutral topic.

- Don't dismiss their interpretation of their symptoms. Show an understanding of what they are sharing. You may have experienced your stress and anxiety in a very different manner.

- Express your concern and offer to help. Ask if they would like help finding some outside support. Ask, "How can I help?" and let them answer. Don't try to "fix" their problem.

We've touched on this next list before. The same things you didn't like to hear you want to avoid saying.

- "Just meditate on it and you'll find a way to deal with it."

- "A change of attitude is what you need."

- "Don't be so negative and down in the mouth. Go out and have some fun, that'll cheer you up."

- "Well, everyone gets the blues sometimes, you'll snap out of it."

- "Sounds like what my cousin had" (and launch into some long tale).

- "Yes, I hear you. Crazy runs in my family too."

Try to avoid doing the following:

- Getting angry because you are frustrated and think they aren't trying hard enough to solve their problem.
- Criticizing them or blaming them for their own situation.
- Don't speak fast or loud. Use pauses to allow them to gather their thoughts and contribute to the conversation.
- Don't assume you really know their situation or things they haven't verified.
- Don't try to make light of the situation and joke them out of their blues. You probably don't have the full picture.
- Watch for patronizing or condescending remarks.

~ A Plan B life can be just as good as or better than a Plan A life. You just have to let go of that first dream and realize that God has already written the first chapter of the new life that awaits you. All you have to do is start reading! ~
- Shannon Alder

Dealing with Setbacks

When you fall off, get right back on the horse. There will not be a "better time" and from past experience, you know that to be true. It is tough, but it's never going to get easier.

It's natural to look around and find something or someone to blame. Blame is a method for convincing yourself that the stress and anxiety you are feeling was brought on by something out of your control. Well, yes. A fender bender where someone else backed into your car is someone else's fault.

The dent in the fender is their fault. The fact that you called in sick two days in a row because you are fretting about repair bills, or having to rent a car, or that your insurance might not cover it and so on is not the fault of the other person. Put your skills to work and take control of the situation rather than blame others.

Depending on what your stressor is, those "others" that you want to blame may be part of your support network. That's classic self-sabotage. Chase everyone away who is there to love and support you. Take a step back and review your past plans and notes. Forget blame and work on a solution to the anxiety.

You feel like you've done everything you can and you just can't beat this one issue. Your ex makes you feel like dirt and no amount of meditation, exercise, or journaling is going to make you feel better and shut off the negative feelings. Time for some outside help. Talk to a trusted friend; find a counselor or a group meeting. You know you can work through this.

Learn from your setback. Figure out why it happened and what you could have done to avoid it, in hindsight. Maybe there was nothing you could have done. It was one of those unexpected triggers (maybe a new one). Now that you know it is there you can be ready to shut it down in the future.

Most of all, you didn't fail. You are not a failure. Life is not a test. The perfect storm of fatigue, doubt, and stress hit you all at once. Forgive yourself, love yourself, and move on.

Annual Checkup

You have an annual checkup for your body, eyes, car, pets, children, and teeth. Why not an annual checkup for your state of mind?

Life is constantly changing and so will your core values or your satisfaction level. You may be in a new job, or a new family situation. Health needs change as we age as well as the needs of your family's health and wellbeing.

Are you happy with where you are in your career, income and personal time? Have you achieved recent goals? Do you have new goals to meet? Have you had any setbacks or has a drama queen popped into your life?

- ***Personal Growth:*** Are you taking chances and trying new things, meeting new people and exploring new places and ideas? Is there anything limiting your ability to grow? How about habits? Have any bad habits crept into your daily routine? Are all of your habits pushing to expand your horizons?

- ***Determination:*** Are you feeling physically and mentally fit. Could you use a boost of energy in the form of a new workout or mental challenge? Are you managing your ability to handle unexpected, unwelcome challenges?

- ***Integrity:*** Does your internal view of yourself match what others see? Are you having troubles keep your promises and following through on completed projects? Do you feel like you are in a good place in your life, or are there something that needs your attention?

- ***Involvement:*** Are you active in your community? Are you helping to make your community better for others? Are you someone who can be counted on?

- ***Recognition:*** Grab your journal - blow the dust off if you must. Write down what you have accomplished in the last twelve months that makes you feel proud of yourself. Now write down what you might have done better or not had time for at all. Is there anyone you need to congratulate or apologize to? If so, write it up in your journal, then write to the actual people. You're not perfect, but you will grow in confidence and credibility if you acknowledge so to yourself and others.

- ***Outreach:*** Are you remembering to thank other people for their help? Recognition of a job well done, which includes showing up on time and ready to work, is always appreciated. You don't know when you might make someone's day just by saying "Thank you, for what you do." Everyone deserves recognition for their input into our society.

- ***Grounding:*** Is there daily or weekly activity that brought you joy in the past, but you simply haven't had time to do it, and you miss it? Get out your calendar and schedule that activity or task. This can happen when you expand your workload and have to concentrate on other things for a while until they become second nature. But take the time to check in and see if you dropped something you really want back. Do whatever it takes to get it back. Even if it's schedule six months out. You know it's there and you can look forward to starting it up again.

Now pull out your old Core Value charge and see if any of the slices need to be changed, or any additions or subtractions to be made. Work through the exercise and see where you stand with your satisfaction rating. You may not have to take it all the way to a fix list or action plan. You will know if you need to do those exercises or not. That's it; I think you are ready for another fantastic year!

Chapter 8: Tools & Exercises

Exercise 1 - Background Survey

- What accomplishments must, in your opinion, occur during your lifetime so that you will consider your life to have been satisfying and well-lived - a life of few or no regrets?

- If there were a secret passion in your life, what would it be?

- How is the most effective way to manage you? Give yourself some tips.

- What is missing in your life? What would make your life more fulfilling?

- What qualities are present in people who inspire you?

- What or who sets you back from achieving your goals? We all have soft spots, times when we feel undeserving or not "good" enough. What is your trigger?

- As your own coach, when you seem to be straying from your goal by procrastinating or self-sabotage, what can you say or does that will help you return to your action plan?

- Exercise is going to be part of your action plan. Do you have a regular exercise routine? Please list.

- Do you have a primary care physician? If not please try to find one, if at all possible.

- Are there any medical issues of which the physician should be aware? Please list.

Exercise 2 - Worry Loop

The Worry	Why	Action	Outcome

Exercise 3 - Mean-Mouth Loop

The Mean Talk	Who was this?	Action	Outcome

Exercise 4 - Core Value Exercise Chart

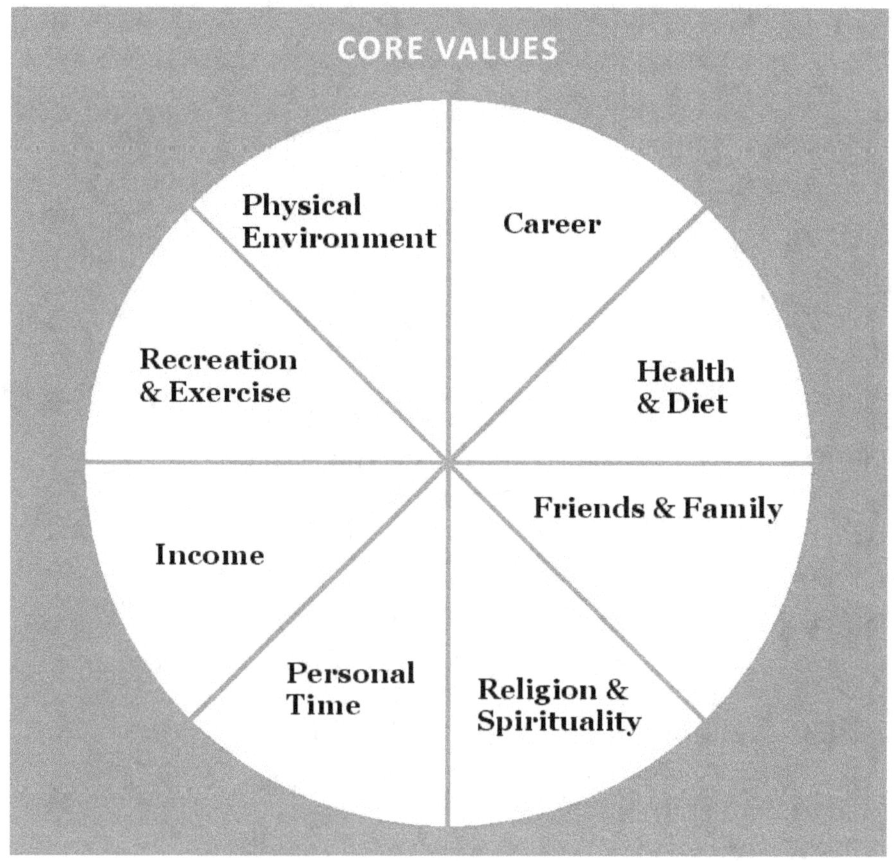

Core Value Word List

Authenticity	Fame
Achievement	Family
Adventure	Friendship
Atmosphere	Fun
Authority	Growth
Autonomy	Happiness
Balance	Health
Beauty	Honesty
Boldness	Humor
Career	Income
Compassion	Influence
Challenge	Inner Harmony
Charity	Justice
Citizenship	Kindness
Community	Knowledge
Competency	Leadership
Contribution	Learning
Creativity	Love
Curiosity	Loyalty
Determination	Meaningful Work
Diet	Openness
Education	Optimism
Environment	Peace
Fairness	Personal Time
Faith	Pleasure

Poise

Popularity

Recognition

Recreation

Religion

Reputation

Respect

Responsibility

Security

Self-respect

Service

Spirituality

Stability

Success status

Trustworthiness

Understanding

Wealth

Wisdom

Exercise 5 - Prompt Words for Health and Recreation

Art
Ballet
Basketball
Badmitten
Baseball
Be positive
Bodysurfing
Boogie board
Canoe
Catnaps
Challenging
Cleaning
Cocktail Parties
Comfortable
Consistent
Creativity
Crew
Cross country skiing
Cycling
Dancing
Dinner Parties
Drawing
Exercycle
Flag football
Focus more on behavior, less on the person.
Focus on good/positive
Free weights
Golf
Gym
Gymnastics
Healthy eating
Home repairs
Honesty
Ice skating
Journaling
Jump rope
Kayak
Kickboxing

Knitting

Fewer carbohydrates

Less fat

Less salt

Less sugar

List

Goals

Meditation

More broiled/baked foods

More music

More raw foods

Needlepoint

No Snacking

Openness

Organized

Pilates

Paint

Ping pong

Play instrument

Play more

Playtime

Play w/family

Play w/pets

Positive reinforcement

Practice good/positive behavior

Quilting

Racketball

Rewards (self)

Relaxed

Rollerblading

Sail surfing

Sailing

Smaller portions

Sing

Skateboard

Skiing – snow

Skiing - water

Skipping

Smile

Snowboard

Sculling

Soccer

Softball

State expectations

Surfing

Swimming

Tae
Kwon Do

Take
classes

Thai Chi

Tennis

Walking

Woodwor
king

Writing

Yoga

Exercise 6 - Prompt Words for Environment

Mauve

Purple

Pink

Beige

Tan

Taupe

Light green

Grass green

Hunter green

Red

Fuchsia

Lemon yellow

Pale yellow

Peacock blue

Sky blue

Pale blue

Orange

Peach

White/black

Rust

House plants

Fish tank

Terrarium

Hanging plants

Gardener

Windchimes

Lawn furniture

Porch

Ceiling fans

Sound system

Upbeat music

Calming music

Comfortable
furniture

Clutter-free

Lived in

Need containers

Clear closets

Recycle old clothes

New bedsheets

Redecorate

Replace appliances

Entertainment
system

Victory garden

Flower garden

Exterior paint

Interior paint

Exterior lighting

Interior lighting

Drapes

Exercise room

Game room

Sit down dinners

Game night

Date night

Bubble baths

Spa day

Exercise 7 - Listing Worries

Type of Worrier:	Over-thinking Loop	Efficiency Problem	Sharing Opportunity	Possible Solutions

Exercise 8 - Prompt Words for Worries

More education/training your you

Better school for children

More education/training for your spouse

Need help with housekeeping

Need help with an elderly family member

Time to read

Time to sleep

Higher salary

Changing careers

Upgrade computer skills

Available jobs

News reports

Checking social media for the bad news

Aging and job opportunities

Savings

Paying for children's education

Purchasing a new car

Repair on the house

Work on social skills

Need to end a relationship

Need to start a relationship

Maintaining the current relationship

Need more friendships

Need some exercise partners

Need someone to hang out with

Would like a travel companion

Health issues - self

Health issues - family

High blood pressure

Diabetes

Overweight

Lack of exercise

Issues with children

Issues with spouse

Exercise 9 - Possible Trigger Prompts

Emotional Triggers	
Interest	Joy
Fear	Sadness
Love	Comfort

	.
Anger	**Guilt**

- Being shouted at
- Forgetting a meeting or appointment
- Thinking about failures
- Thinking about your significant other
- Watching children play
- Thinking about family vacation
- An invitation to a cocktail party
- Thinking about a past trauma
- Experiencing failures
- Experiencing success
- Being mocked or criticized
- Being excluded
- Hearing music - what kind?
- Thinking about being underwater

- Thinking about being alone

- Losing a job

- Walking on a crowded city street

- Starting a new project

- First time at a club meeting

- Eating a new cuisine

- Walking alone in the woods

- First day on a new job

- Being asked to figure out something complicated

- Having your authority challenged

- Where is your scary place?

- Hurting someone's feelings

- Being betrayed

- Lying to someone

- Walking through a garden

- Eating in a new restaurant

Exercise 10 - Analysis Loop Exercise

	Analysis Loop - Why are you looping through this particular discussion?
Who:	
What:	
Outcome:	
Feelings:	
Desired Outcome:	

Exercise 11 - Example Chart for Better Habits

Keeping Your Space Clean		
Name	Date	New Habit

Conclusion

Thank you for making it through to the end of *Stop Overthinking: Tools to Improve Your Quality of Life*, let's hope it was informative and able to provide you with all of the tools you need to achieve your goals whatever they may be.

The next step is to enjoy your life along with the lives of the friends and family around you to the fullest. Keep your finger on the pulse of your emotions. You know when to determine if you need to fire up the journaling or run a few looping exercises to make sure you haven't slipped back into some old habits. We have put quite a few coping techniques at your disposal to help you move onward and upward toward your goals.

I hope you will share what you have learned with friends, family, and coworkers so that they may benefit from what you have learned. A gift of coping strategies for your children to use when they are faced with bullies or disappointments is one of the best things you could possibly do for them.

Look at all the words that describe you now: trustworthy, loving, motivated, happy, joyful, accepting, calm, courage under fire, levelheaded, safe, competent, confident, successful, and entertaining.

Congratulations again for your continuing hard work. Keep building the life you want while helping others achieve their goals as well.

Finally, if you found this book useful in any way, a review on Amazon is always appreciated!